Derbyshire Walks with Children

William D. Parke

Published by Sigma Leisure – an imprint of
Sigma Press, 1 South Oak Lane, Wilmslow, Cheshire SK9 6AR, England.

British Library Cataloguing in Publication Data
A CIP record for this book is available from the British Library.

ISBN: 1-85058-613-6

First published 1997, Reprinted 1999.

Typesetting and Design by: Sigma Press, Wilmslow, Cheshire.

Cover photograph: The Stepping Stones, Dovedale (Gail M. Parke)

Maps: William D. Parke

Photographs: Gail M. Parke

Printed by: MFP Design & Print

Disclaimer: the information in this book is given in good faith and is believed to be correct at the time of publication. No responsibility is accepted by either the author or publisher for errors or omissions, or for any loss or injury howsoever caused. Only you can judge your own fitness, competence and experience.

Preface

Derbyshire to the majority of people is synonymous with the Peak District with its outstanding scenery and splendid walking country. The Peak District, however, is only part of Derbyshire and there are several other areas of the county that offer both interest and enjoyable walking. The twenty-four walks described in this book provide the opportunity for parents and their children to experience the full range of the county's diverse countryside. Stunning heather-covered moors and mountain scenery dominate North Derbyshire, whilst the west has its limestone hills and dales and a glistening pattern of drystone walls. The area's clear streams and rivers provide some of the finest fishing in England and ancient, picturesque, stone villages abound. South Derbyshire offers a more tranquil landscape of timber-framed, brick and often thatched houses set in rich, rolling farmland bisected by the powerful River Trent. The eastern part of the county, although highly developed for housing and industry, has many oases that provide a more rural and timeless view of Derbyshire.

The walks reflect the needs of a young family where the children's ages, interests and walking abilities will be diverse. They should maintain the youngsters' interest, provide an enjoyable learning experience and encourage walking as a lifelong means of achieving health and relaxation. The complaint, "Walking is boring," should be a thing of the past.

I have checked and rechecked all the route descriptions, but nature and man continually alter the landscape. Gates become stiles, trees disappear from the landscape and hedges and walls are altered. The route maps provide a rough guide to each walk but you should also carry the appropriate Ordnance Survey map. Ordnance Survey maps, apart from ensuring that you can check your location, provide a great opportunity to get your children interested in map-reading. Let them find their location on the map and learn how map-makers interpret the landscape and its features. The availability of a compass also adds to the enjoyment and interest.

Most of the walks list places for refreshment. This is fine, but to maintain the spirit of the great outdoors consider having a picnic. There are many splendid picnic sites along the routes. However, remember that many of the creatures that you will see on your walks would also like to share your feast!

Finally, I hope that you and your children will enjoy these walks as much as my family and I have.

William D. Parke

Contents

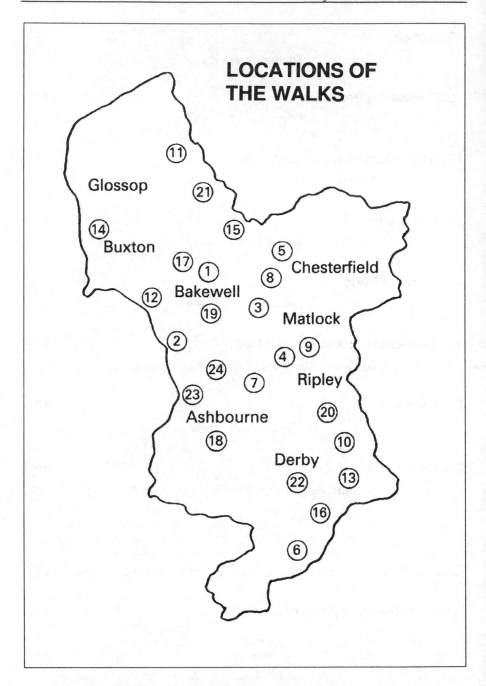

LOCATIONS OF
THE WALKS

Before you begin

Please consider the following points which, when followed, should increase your enjoyment of walking in Derbyshire.

☆ Do not climb drystone walls except where a stile is provided. Damaged walls can allow farm animals to stray. Wall repair is labour intensive and expensive - remember the aim is to have the landowner as the walker's friend.

☆ Having used a gate, please close, and where relevant, secure it. Open gates are another means by which farm animals can stray, perhaps even into the path of vehicles.

☆ Take your litter home with you or deposit in a bin. Litter is not only unsightly, but can also cause injury.

☆ Remember all animals are nervous of man. Wild animals in particular if frightened may bite and all mothers are protective of their young. Be aware of these facts and act accordingly. If feeding horses, ponies, etc., offer the food in the palm of your hand so that the do not take your fingers as well!

☆ Respect private land and do not stray from Public Rights of Way or concessionary paths. Leaving the designated route can damage crops, disturb wildlife and possibly endanger your safety in quarrying/mining areas. Persistent trespass may lead to route closure.

☆ Avoid disturbing nesting birds, particularly those that make theirs nests in heather or amongst reeds.

☆ Take nothing home with you except your experience of the walk. The countryside and particularly its rare plants should be left for all to enjoy.

☆ Do not set fire to the countryside. Be aware that after a prolonged dry spell, moorland in particular can become tinder dry with a high risk of being set alight. Fires can be caused by discarding glass or hot objects, as well as by open flames.

☆ Protect water sources. Avoid their pollution.

☆ Swimming, paddling and all activities on or close to water should be supervised. Depths, currents and below surface conditions are all questionable. Watch out for mooring rings and keep clear of mooring ropes.

☆ When walking on roads, keep well into the side and in single file. Roads are not play areas.

☆ Fungi and berries can look very attractive but they should not be eaten as some are deadly poisonous.

☆ Dogs should always be kept under strict control and on a lead whilst on a road or passing farm animals. Leads must be used at lambing time and on "access land".

☆ Finally, respect the tranquillity of the countryside - which is one of its main attractions.

A Note about Public Rights of Way

Public Rights of Way are considered to be part of the Queen's Highway and as such are protected in law. They are recorded by the Highway Authority (Derbyshire County Council 01629 580000) on definitive maps which are open for inspection. The surface of the right of way is owned by the Highway Authority, which has the obligation to ensure freedom of passage by, in the case of a Public Footpath, pedestrians and their natural accompaniment (a dog under close control, a pushchair, a pram etc.). It is illegal to obstruct a right of way (dense undergrowth is not considered to be an obstruction), to plough up the surface of a right of way which does not cross a field (those that cross a field can be ploughed if it would be impractical to lift the plough but the surface must be restored by the farmer within two weeks), to sow a crop (other than grass) on a right of way, to erect a misleading notice (anything that implies that the right of way does not exist), or to divert/close a right of way without due legal process.

If you come across an obstruction, you have the right to clear it by the minimum degree required to permit passage. You have the right to follow the line of the right of way across any crops growing on it.

Any obstruction, illegal diversion or closure, defective stiles/gates/bridges or difficulties, including dense undergrowth and/or impassable mud, should be reported to the Highway Authority and the Ramblers' Association (RA). The address for the RA is: **The Ramblers' Association, 1/5 Wandsworth Road, London SW8 2XX**

Public Transport

Railway timetable and fare information is available by calling 0345 484950. Bus route timetable and fare information is available from Derbyshire County Council BUSLINE on: Buxton, 01246 250450; Derby

01332 292200; Chesterfield 01246 250450 - daily between 0700 hours and 2000 hours.

Tourist Information Centres

The telephone numbers of the major Tourist Information Centres are as follows:
Derby: 01332 255802
Ashbourne: 01335 343666
Matlock Bath: 01629 55082
Bakewell: 01629 813227
Chesterfield: 01246 207777
Buxton: 01298 25106

Introductory Notes on the Text

This is a very unusual book, intended to be read by both parents and children. The following conventions have been used to make the book as useful as possible to both categories:

Directions are numbered and appear in bold text so that they can be seen at a glance.

☺ Information for the children is set in a contrasting typestyle. This is to be read aloud, or for them to read themselves. **OTHER INFORMATION FOR PARENTS APPEARS IN BOLD CAPITALS.**

Questions (and answers) are in the same type style, with "Q" and "A".

In between the instructions you will often see text that looks like this. We have used this for all sorts of extra information, ranging from background material to escape routes – generally, the sort of thing you can skate over if you are in a rush to complete the main walk.

Checklists appear at the end of each walk, for the children to tick off things as they see them. If you do not want to write in the book, copy the checklist onto a piece of paper, and give one to each child, so that they can compete to see who spots the most.

Sketch maps

The maps are intended only as a rough guide to the route and are not drawn to scale. Unless otherwise stated, North is upwards. Not all buildings are shown.

Roads	=	a continuous line
Footpaths	=	a dotted line
P	=	parking
PH	=	public house
PC	=	public convenience

Quick Reference Chart

Plan your day at a glance, and check which routes have the features or facilities you require. For more information, see the individual route.

Notes and key

Rail:	routes that are within a short walk of a railway station
Bus:	routes that are within in short walk from a bus stop
Café:	café or tea room along the route or within easy walking distance
Pubs:	pubs along the route where families are welcome, with seats outside or a family room
Wet Weather	walks suitable for bad weather or winter conditions, usually with gravelled paths or all-weather surfaces
Flat:	route is more or less flat, or can be made flat using escape routes ●● = totally flat circular route
Historical:	place(s) of historical interest features along the route, or close by
Pushchairs:	walks with at least a small route suitable for pushchairs, though it may involve some effort ●● = complete circular routes that are totally suitable, or can be made suitable, for pushchairs
Features:	places of specific interest to children along the route or close-by

	Rail	Bus	Café	Pubs	Wet Weather	Flat	Historical	Push-chairs	Features
1. Bakewell		●	●	●			Various	●	Well dressing, museum, packhorse bridges
2. Beresford		●	●	●					Caves and Nature Reserve
3. Birchover		●		●			Bronze age site		Stone circle and huge climbing stones
4. Black Rocks		●					Old Railway & lead mine	●	Woods and large outcrop of rocks
5. Blackstone		●		●					Hilltop monuments highland cattle
6. Calke Abbey		●	●	●		●	Stately home		Deer, lakes and lime kilns
7. Carsington		●	●		●	●●		●●	Cycle and boat hire, bird hides
8. Chatsworth		●	●				Stately Home		Children's farmyard and adventure playground
9. Cromford	●	●	●		●		Cotton Mill, old railway		Canal and pumping house
10. Dale Abbey		●	●	●		●●	Abbey ruins	●	Hermit's caves
11. Derwent Res.		●	●				World War II Dambusters' training site		Dams, cycle hire, woods and birds
12. Earl Sterndale		●		●					
13. Elvaston		●	●		●	●●	Country estate	●●	Cycle Hire and working museum
14. Goyt Valley								●	Old packhorse bridge, moors and streams
15. Longshaw		●	●	●			Grouse moors old millstone quarries	●	Iron age fort and massive rocks
16. Melbourne		●	●	●		●	Church, hall and gardens	●	Wildfowl
17. Monsal Dale		●	●	●			Old railway		Weir and railway viaduct
18. Osmaston		●		●			Country Estate estate village		Birds, woods and lakes
19. Over Haddon		●	●						Ancient bridges and fords
20. Shipley Park		●	●		●	●	Country estate	●●	Wildfowl and mining relics
21. Stanage Edge		●							Moors and cliffs
22. Swarkestone		●	●	●		●●	1745 rebellion	●	Canal and lock
23. Thorpe Cloud		●		●					Stepping stones
24. Tissington		●				●	Estate Village and manor house	●	Well dressing

1. Bakewell and Ashford in The Water

Bakewell is the major town of the Peak District and is set in an area of outstanding natural beauty. This walk takes you through its historic and picturesque streets and along the River Wye to Ashford, another Derbyshire gem. The return is mostly along the trackbed of the old London to Manchester via Derby railway. Provides just the appetite for a Bakewell Pudding!

Starting point:	Rutland Square, Bakewell (SK217 685). This is the point where the A6 (London to Carlisle trunk road) meets the road to Sheffield and Chesterfield. There are car parks throughout the lower town, the market and across the river off Coombes Road.
By bus:	Services from Sheffield, Chesterfield, Derby, Buxton, Stoke on Trent and Manchester.
Distance:	Entire route 5¾ miles. Shorter route 3½ miles. Town route 1 mile.
Terrain:	Mainly riverside footpaths and a walking trail along the bed of a dismantled railway. Some pavement walking. It may be muddy between points 6 and 7 and at point 14.
Maps:	OS Outdoor Leisure Sheet 24
Public Toilets:	In the car park behind the information centre, Bridge Street, Bakewell and in the car park at Ashford.
Refreshments:	Numerous cafés, restaurants and tea rooms in Bakewell. The Bull's Head and Devonshire Arms pubs and cafés in Ashford.
Pushchairs:	The "town" route is suitable for pushchairs providing that the "Scott's Gardens" section is circumvented by following the perimeter pavement.

☺ **(OUTSIDE THE RUTLAND ARMS HOTEL)** This Hotel was built in 1804 on the site of The White Horse Inn. Both were coaching inns on the stage route between Derby and Manchester. The author Jane Austen stayed at the hotel and Bakewell features in her novel *Pride and Prejudice* disguised as Lambton. It was in this hotel that the Bakewell Pudding was first made. In 1859 the hotel cook's assistant misunderstood her instructions for making a dessert. The result was delicious and you can buy freshly baked puddings from a number of shops in the town.

1. With your back to the Rutland Arms Hotel, walk the length of Rutland Square, passing, on your right, the Bakewell Pudding Shop. Continue ahead via the one way street (oncoming traffic) known as Bridge Street, past the 17th-century market hall (now an information centre) to Bakewell Bridge.

☺ Picturesque Bakewell Bridge has provided the crossing of the River Wye for over 600 years and is one of the oldest in the country. The river and its banks are home to extremely tame ducks and geese which often stop the traffic as they wander across or even just sit down on the nearby roads. You will gain many a friend with a little food!

2. Cross the bridge, turn left through a metal gate into Scott's Gardens, and then follow the riverside path upstream to a gate. Pass through this and another to follow the path diagonally left across the meadow.

☺ In Scott's Gardens you will often find horses, cattle, or sheep grazing. The sheep are usually in the first meadow next to Bakewell Bridge and they thoroughly enjoy raiding picnics.

3. At the far side of the meadows pass through a gate, turn left onto Holme Lane and follow it to Holme Bridge.

☺ This is Holme Packhorse Bridge which was rebuilt in 1664. It is only 1.25 metres wide, and was used to avoid Bakewell Market where charges (tolls) would have been made for all goods passing through.

Q: Why are the bridge walls so low?

A: They allowed for free movement of the goods carried on the backs of the packhorses.

Escape Route: Instead of turning left onto the bridge, turn right and follow the lane upwards to the left of Holme Hall. This becomes a track and passes through an old quarry to a field gate. Once through the

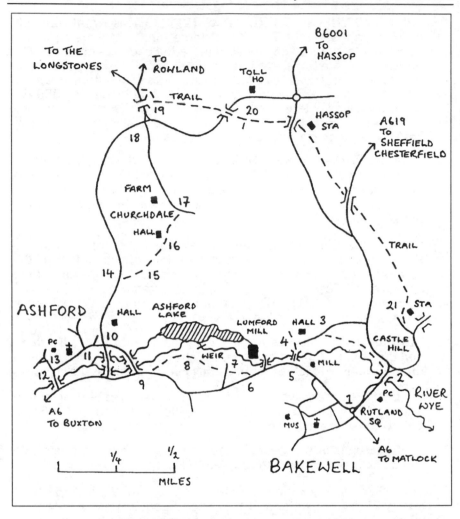

gate, again follow the track but when it turns left you should continue up
the field to a stile. Cross this and now follow the path straight ahead
over the summit and down to the Monsal Trail. Turn right onto the trail
and follow the main route description from point 20.

☺ The route that you are following from Holme Bridge is an old
   packhorse route. The quarry at the start of the climb was a churt
   mine. This is a flint-hard stone which was crushed to a powder
   and transported to Stoke on Trent for use in the manufacture of
   porcelain – it makes the porcelain white. The high ground of this

route is home to many birds. Look out for skylarks as they hang in the air and sing non-stop, and swallows and lapwings with their green backs and black crests. You should also see flowers such as harebells (Scottish bluebell), wild thyme and stonecrop.

4. Cross the bridge and follow the stone-flagged path to the A6.

☺ At the far end of the bridge there is a pen which was used when sheep were washed in the river. Here also is the mill stream for the 19th-century Victoria Corn Mill which last ground corn in the 1940s. You should be able to see part of the mill from here. It is the three-storey building 30 metres to your left along the main road. Victoria Mill is believed to have been built on the site of the original corn mill for Bakewell. In 1086 it was valued at 10s 8d (approximately 53 new pence) – a great deal of money in those days.

Town Route: Turn left on to the A6 and walk past the fire station and Victoria Mill to reach the first turning on your right (Bagshaw Hill). Take this road, which climbs steeply past Bagshaw Hall (on your right) to a road junction at the Gospel Hall (on your left). Here turn half left onto Church Lane and, immediately after the house on your left, go through a squeezer stile into the church yard. Follow the path in an anti-clockwise direction around the church. At the church's south entrance (flag pole), turn right and walk down into South Church Street. Turn left and follow the road downhill into Rutland Square.

☺ **(IN THE CHURCHYARD)** There has been a church on this spot for over a thousand years. At the south-west corner you will find some ancient stone coffins with the shapes of human figures carved into them. Notice the sundial above the south-west entrance and the 2.5 metre high Saxon cross (9th-century) just past the south entrance. Can you see the little animal nibbling some leaves?

☺ **(JUST AFTER CHURCH ALLEY)** The buildings on your left are almshouses known as St John's Hospital. They date from 1709 and were built to house six poor, single men. Next door is the Old Town Hall and Courtroom built in 1602. On the top of the building there is a bell which was used to summon the fire engine.

5. Here turn right and follow the river upstream to the next bridge, which gives access to Lumford Mill.

☺ This is Lumford Mill which was originally a cotton spinning factory. It employed about 300 people, mainly women and children, turning American cotton into yarn. The mill burnt down and was partly replaced in 1868. After cotton spinning it was used to make electric batteries, particularly those used in submarines during the Second World War.

6. **Continue along the A6 and after the last factory turn right through a squeezer stile. Follow the field path diagonally left and between houses to a road.**

☺ There are often horses in this field which are usually to be found at the roadside wall watching all that goes by. They are grateful for the odd sugar lump, carrot or apple.

7. **Cross the road, pass between more houses and then follow the clear path across a series of small fields to emerge above a small, dry valley.**

☺ **(ON REACHING THE DRY VALLEY, POINT OUT THE WEIR TO YOUR RIGHT)** This weir and the lakes that it maintains were built to produce enough water to drive the two waterwheels at Lumford Mill. When the river is in flood the weir is very impressive with its tumbling white water.

8. **Cross the dry valley and climb up the opposing slope, keeping parallel with the river. In a short while the path descends and crosses the meadows to a kissing gate.**

☺ Ducks and geese often wander these meadows, but look for other wildfowl, particularly along the wooded part of the river's opposite bank.

9. **Pass through the gate and turn right to reach a road. Then turn right again, cross two bridges and follow the road to its junction with the A6020.**

☺ **(AT THE SECOND BRIDGE)** Standing at this peaceful spot it is hard to believe that until 1931 this was the main road between London, Carlisle and south-west Scotland. If you look over the downstream bridge wall you will often find both brown and rainbow trout swimming in the clear water.

Q: What is inscribed on the bridge wall that you have just been leaning on?

A: "M. HYDE 1664." It is in memory of the Reverend Hyde, the vicar of Bakewell, who was here thrown from his horse and drowned in the river.

10. Cross the A6020 and pass the post office to reach the road junction outside the Ashford Hotel.

Q: Opposite the post office you should see a cast iron milepost. What is the distance to London?

A: 154 miles.

☺ The road opposite the Ashford Hotel is called Greaves Lane. "Greaves" was the name given to the waste tallow from candle manufacture. To confirm that they were made here you have only to look for Candle House in this lane.

☺ Ashford has six wells and they are dressed (decorated) in thanksgiving for their waters each year around Trinity Sunday. Two of them (Greaves Lane Well and The Little Well) are in Greaves Lane.

11. From the Ashford Hotel walk along Church Street to the market stance.

☺ On your left, just after the Ashford Hotel, you should see Great Batch Well and another well is within the market stance.

12. Turn left at the market stance to Sheepwash Bridge.

☺ This is a 17th-century packhorse bridge. An information board explains how sheep were washed here, and demonstrations are given around Trinity Sunday. The packhorses carried malt from Derby and up to 300 used to cross the bridge in any one week.

13. Retrace your steps back to the post office. Now turn left onto the Old Baslow Road, and left again when this meets the A6020.

14. At the left-hand bend, cross the road WITH EXTREME CARE to a squeezer stile. Pass through this and over a brook to a hand gate. Now follow the path as it bears left, up and along the slope to a stile.

Q: As you walk up the slope you will pass underneath a large tree. What type of tree is it?

A: A Horse Chestnut, and in the autumn the ground here is covered with conkers.

15. Cross the stile, maintaining your direction, and then another to reach a wall stile beside a field gate.

☺ As you cross these fields a wonderful, panoramic view opens up.

Sheepwash Bridge, Ashford in the Water

The long ridge to the north is known as Longstone Edge, 1295feet (395metres). For many years it was the scene of intensive lead mining, with the ore-bearing vein running the length of the ridge.

16. **Cross the stile, bear left and follow the path which skirts the field in front of Church Dale Hall to reach a roadside stile.**

Q: What is the ditch in front of the garden called?

A: It is known as a "Ha-Ha". It provides a barrier to animals, but cannot be seen from the house and is named from the surprise that it gives when discovered.

17. **Cross the stile, then turn left on to the road and follow it past Church Dale Farm to the A6020.**

☺ **(ON CROSSING THE STILE)** In spring the woodland and roadsides here are a sea of daffodils. At the same time the fields are full of lambs which jump around as if they were on springs. Notice the water trough in front of Church Dale Farm which is carved from a single piece of gritstone.

18. **Cross over the junction and follow the Great Longstone and Rowland**

Road under the bridge to a road fork. Here take the path on the right up to the Monsal Trail.

Q: What is the clearance beneath the bridge?

A: 12 feet 3 inches (4 metres).

☺ The walking and cycling trail that you are about to follow is known as the Monsal Trail. Before 1968 it was a twin track railway used by mainline trains between London and Manchester. It is now difficult to imagine that two huge steam trains could speed past each other on this trackbed.

19. **Turn left on to the trail and follow it for approximately 800 metres to where a footpath crosses the old trackbed.**

☺ The sides of the old railway are slowly being recovered by nature. Along the cuttings and embankments you should find many wild flowers, one of which is the bloody cranesbill. It looks like a geranium and gains its name from the fruit which looks like the bill of the crane bird. Pheasants and rabbits come and go all over the place.

20. *(The escape route rejoins here).* **Continue along the trail for approximately 1¼ miles to old Bakewell Station.**

☺ Where a footpath crosses the trail, look to your left and you will see an isolated house along the A6020 road. It is called Toll Bar House and a visual play on those words can be seen just below the roof. This is where tolls or fees were charged for the use of the road in the 18th and 19th centuries. A bar was placed across the road to ensure that no cart or horse passed without payment.

☺ **(AT THE FIRST RAILWAY STATION)** This was Hassop Station, but now houses a book shop. It was built in 1862 but it was little used by passengers. At the time Hassop had a population of only 100 people, and the planned rail links to Sheffield never happened.

Q: As you pass under the next bridge (Pineapple Bridge), can you identify the cause of the black marks on its roof?

A: They are the soot marks from steam trains.

☺ **(AT THE SECOND STATION)** This is Bakewell Station which, unlike the one at Hassop, had a large passenger business, particularly during the annual Bakewell show. Freight traffic was halted during the show and excursion trains arrived from the West Midlands, Nottingham, Manchester and Yorkshire. The show still takes place today, but now everyone arrives by road!.

21. **Turn right to cross the old station yard and then left along the road to a junction. Bear right and follow Station Road downhill to Bakewell Bridge. Cross this and retrace your earlier route to Rutland Square.**

Other Places of Interest in the Area

The Old House Museum, Cunningham Place, Bakewell

The museum is housed in a building which dates from 1534. Period interior including a vast, open fireplace. Exhibitions and displays on local occupations (operate the bellows in a blacksmith's shop), domestic life, photography, toys, lace, costumes etc. Telephone 01629 813165 for opening dates and times.

Bakewell and Ashford Checklist

- [ ] A WAR MEMORIAL
- [ ] A STONE WATER TROUGH
- [ ] A CHURCH SPIRE
- [ ] DUCKS
- [ ] A HORSE
- [ ] PHEASANTS
- [ ] TROUT
- [ ] A WELL
- [ ] A FIRE STATION TOWER
- [ ] A RED CROSS

2. Beresford, Wolfscote and Biggin Dales

This circular walk from the picturesque village of Hartington provides a memorable experience. The scenery is constantly changing – pasture gives way to a gorge, which is succeeded in turn by meadow, scree-covered valleys and then limestone upland with its drystone-walled fields. A visual delight with interest at every turn.

Starting point: The Warslow Road car park, Hartington (SK127 603). Hartington is 11 miles south-east of Buxton. Follow the A515 in the direction of Ashbourne and after approximately 10½ miles, turn right on to the B5054. Follow this through Hartington and you will see the car park to your right as you approach the edge of the village.

By bus: Service from Buxton (no Sunday Service in winter). Leave the Square by the Warslow Road and shortly you will see (on your left) the toilets and pottery mentioned in point 1.

Distance: Entire route 5¾ miles. Shorter route 3 miles.

Terrain: Limestone grassland and valley paths – parts are purpose-made, all-weather surfaces. Some country lane walking, but with little or no traffic.

Maps: OS Outdoor Leisure Sheet 24.

Public Toilets: Warslow Road, Hartington – diagonally left across the road from the car park entrance.

Refreshments: Charles Cotton Hotel, Devonshire Arms pub and cafés, Hartington.

Pushchairs: Unsuitable

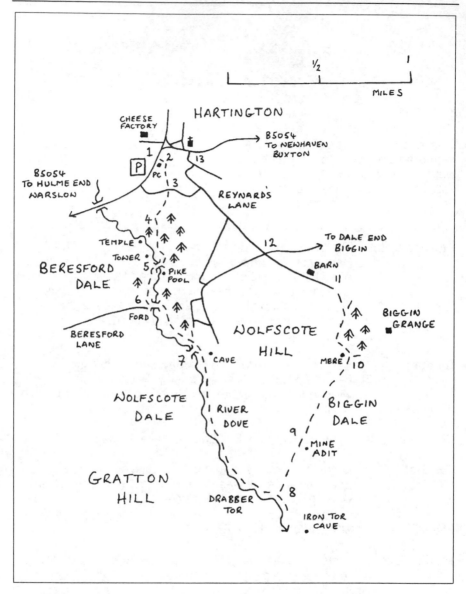

1. **Return to the car park entrance and turn left onto Warslow Road. Follow this for approximately 30 metres to reach the public toilets that are set back on the right-hand side of the road. Turn right and follow the path between the toilets and a pottery to a hand gate.**

Q: At the beginning of the path there is a green, cast-iron footpath sign. When was it made?

A: 1907. It is one of a number of such signs to be found in North Derbyshire. The signs give the altitude at which they lie! This one is at 758 feet (231 metres) above sea level.

2. **Pass through the gate and follow the path, which bears right to run along the left-hand side of a drystone wall. After 200 metres the path passes through a wall gap and then continues for a further 100 metres to a wall stile.**

☺ The fields through which you are passing are typical limestone grazing areas. The grass is very short and grows on a thin layer of soil. Limestone rock breaks through the surface in may places. These fields are usually grazed by horses, which take a great interest in walkers, especially their picnics!

☺ After passing through the wall gap, look at the surface of the fields on your right. They have long ridges and furrows which indicate that they were ploughed in ancient times.

3. **Cross the stile, the enclosed lane and the opposing stile to follow the well- worn path across three grazing fields. The path is marked by a series of posts.**

☺ As you reach the highest point in the third grazing field, you should see a river to your right. This is the River Dove which forms the county boundary with Staffordshire.

Q: What is the name of the thorn bushes or small trees that grow alongside the path?

A: They are hawthorns. The maroon-coloured berries that they bear in the autumn and winter are the haws.

4. **At the end of the grazing land, pass through a gated squeezer stile to enter the woods of Beresford Dale. Follow the clearly defined path down to the River Dove and along its banks to a footbridge.**

☺ As you approach the woods look down towards the river and you should see a small square-shaped building on the Staffordshire bank. This is known as The Fishing Temple (unfortunately, the public cannot visit the building as it lies on private land). It was built in 1674 by Charles Cotton, who lived nearby, for when he and his friend Izaak Walton, fished here. It is well known to fishermen all over the world as these men wrote the famous book

The Compleat Angler and considered this to be their favourite fishing spot. See if you can see trout which are descended from those which gave such sport over 300 years ago.

☺ After the temple, the great limestone cliffs of Beresford Dale rise from both sides of the river. Can you see the tower atop the cliffs on the opposite bank? This is all that remains of Beresford Hall, the home of Charles Cotton.

5. **Cross the bridge and continue along the river bank to another bridge.**

☺ Immediately after crossing the bridge there is a deep pool known as Pike Pool. It receives its name from the spire of rock rather than from the fish.

☺ As the dale opens out you should see and hear many birds amongst the trees and along the river itself. Look particularly for nature's fisherman – the blue heron. The bank here and further downstream is often covered with little heaps of soil which show the tunnelling activities of the mole.

6. **Cross the bridge, bear right and follow the path across the meadow to a wall stile next to the river. Continue along the bankside path, for approximately 30 metres, to reach a squeezer stile.**

☺ **(AT THE FIRST FOOTBRIDGE)** This is Beaver's Ford. Notice the stepping stones which were the means of crossing on foot before the wooden bridge was built.

Escape route: Without passing through the squeezer stile, turn left and climb the enclosed track. Ignore the first turning to the right, but when the track turns right, follow it to a road. Turn left on to the road and then take the next left, which is another track. In approximately half a mile you should reach a T-junction. Here turn left onto Reynard's Lane and rejoin the main route. See point 12.

7. **Pass through the squeezer to enter Wolfscote Dale and follow the river bank path for approximately 1¼ miles to the second squeezer stile.**

☺ You should see from the National Trust sign that you are now in Wolfscote Dale. Up your left is *Frank i' th' Rocks* cave which is worth careful exploration. The dale itself, unlike the previous one, cuts a perfect 'V' through the hills, which climb to around 1200 feet (365 metres). In many places the rocks have broken away from the hillsides and formed an avalanche of small stones known as "scree". If you look amongst the scree you may find the

Wolfscote Dale

fossilised remains of the millions and millions of sea creatures that formed these limestone hills 300 million years ago.

Q: Can you recognise the trees that grow along the riverbank? Each year they produce catkins and their seeds are borne within small egg-shaped cones. The black empty cones from previous years remain, until detached by the wind and rain.

A: They are alders.

☺ **(INDICATE THE GREAT STONE BUTTRESS OF DRABBER TOR WHICH APPEARS ABOVE THE OPPOSITE BANK, APPROXIMATELY 1 MILE ALONG THE RIVER)** The large rock buttress above the opposite bank is known as Drabber Tor. It and the rock buttresses that follow it (Peasland Rocks) are the remains of coral reefs.

8. Without passing through the squeezer, turn left and follow the stony path up Biggin Dale to reach, in approximately a quarter of a mile, a stile on your right.

☺ This is Biggin Dale which, apart from the odd damp patch and spring, no longer has a surface water course. It is therefore known as a dry valley. The dale has the feel of the wilderness. In places trees appear to grow from the bare rocks and birds of prey can be seen hovering above its slopes.

☺ The cave on your right, across the stile, has been made by man. It is the entrance to an old lead mine where the thin vein of lead ore (galena) has been followed for about 50 metres.

9. **Continue up the dale to reach, in approximately two thirds of a mile, a gate giving access to a National Nature Reserve. Pass through the gate and again continue up the dale, until reaching a mere where a side valley enters from the right.**

☺ The National Nature Reserve contains very rare alpine plants — look, but do not pick. In season a variety of butterflies can be seen here, but the most striking feature is the bright yellow flowers of the dark green, prickly gorse or furze bushes.

10. **Turn left around the mere, pass through a gate and then bear right to continue up Biggin Dale. In 150 metres, when a footpath sign appears on your right, turn left (signposted Hartington) and walk up to a field gate.**

11. **Pass through the gate and follow the green lane to reach, in approximately half a mile, a crossroads.**

☺ This type of lane is called a green lane as it does not have a stone or tarmac surface. It is often covered in grass and other vegetation. This is how most country lanes looked before the coming of the motor car. Such lanes would only have boot and horseshoe marks, and the ruts made by wagon wheels.

Q: You will pass a very old barn made from the local limestone and weathered grey. What are the metal crosses in the two end walls for?

A: They are connected through the length of the building by metal rods and hold the walls together. With age, the end walls are no longer upright. They have bowed and without the metal supports would collapse.

12. **Pass straight across the crossroads and follow Reynard's Lane for approximately three quarters of a mile to a T-junction in Hartington.** *(The escape route rejoins from the first turning on your left).*

☺ The walk along Reynard's Lane provides a wonderful view of the

Dove Valley. If you have an Ordnance Survey map, see if you can identify the view's features on it.

13. **Turn left down to another T-junction and left again to reach the centre of Hartington. Follow the B5054 in the direction of Hulme End to shortly return to the car park.**

☺ The duck pond is home to mallard, domestic and muscovy ducks. The muscovy is more like a turkey in size and mostly black with a large, rather ugly, red beak. The ducks wander all over the village and are always looking for the odd crumb.

☺ The little cheese shop beside the pond sells straight from the dairy-factory located to its rear. Around Hartington you will often see the green and yellow milk tankers of the dairy with the words "Derbyshire Milk for Hartington Stilton" written on them. Stilton is a type of cheese which can only be called by that name if made in certain English counties, of which Derbyshire is one.

Beresford, Wolfscote and Biggin Dales Checklist

☐ A YEW

☐ A WEIR

☐ A MERE

☐ AN ALDER

☐ A HERON

☐ STEPPING STONES

☐ A CHURCH TOWER

☐ A MILK TANKER

☐ A BIRD OF PREY

☐ A TOWER

3. Birchover and Stanton Moor

Stanton Moor is the heather-covered plateau immediately to the south-west of the Derwent and Wye river confluence. At just over 1000 feet (305 metres) it provides extensive views. The moor is covered with Bronze Age relics including a circle of nine standing stones and massive isolated stones with climbing holes cut into them. Birchover village nestles on the hillside below the moor and is mainly involved in quarrying. The quarries are hardly noticeable on this route but what is seen, in fact, adds interest.

Starting point: Outside the Red Lion Inn, Birchover (SK236 622). Birchover is 6 miles south-east of Bakewell. Take the A6 towards Matlock and after approximately 3 miles turn right onto the B5056. Birchover is signposted to the left after a further 2 miles. Unfortunately, cars can only be parked on the village roads. Please show due consideration for others.

By bus: Services from Bakewell and Matlock (no Sunday service)

Distance: Entire route 3 miles

Terrain: Mostly moor and woodland paths. A little walking along a country road.

Maps: OS Outdoor Leisure Sheet 24

Public Toilets: Main Street, Birchover

Refreshments: Red Lion and Druid Inns, Birchover

Pushchairs: Unsuitable

---

1.   **From the Red Lion Inn, walk down the street to the Druid Inn.**

☺ "Birchover" means "birch-covered bank", and during this walk you will see many of those trees with their silver bark. The village is mainly concerned with quarrying fine pink gritstone and the manufacture of grinding and millstones.

(A small detour to Rowter Rocks is highly recommended. Follow the lane

to the left of the Druid Inn and immediately after those premises you will find a gap in the wall that gives access to the rocks.)

☺ This massive pile of rocks, which in places rises to 45 metres, is known as Rowter Rocks. In the 18th century, seats, rooms and stairs were carved into these rocks by the Rev Thomas Eyre — see what you can discover. Over the years a tale was formed that all of this work had been carried out by the Druids, hence the name of the inn here.

2. **On the bend opposite the Druid Inn, turn right onto a path that leads uphill. This passes through trees above the village to reach a quarry car park.**

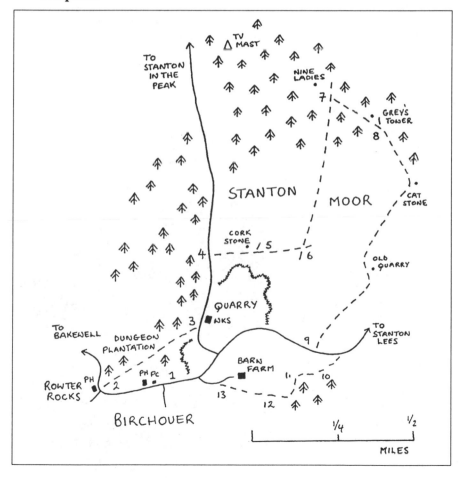

Q: What type of tree mainly lines this path?

A: The sycamore. Notice that the leaves have black spots that are only to be found in country areas.

3.   Pass through the car park and turn left onto the road. Follow this for a quarter of a mile, until you reach a footpath on your right. The footpath has a walled entrance.

☺ At the Ann Twyford Dimensional Stone quarry you should see some of the pink gritstone that has been cut from the rock face. This is one of a few quarries that also produce grinding and millstones. The stone is hard enough to put an edge on steel!

4.   Turn right and follow the path to a stile. Cross this onto Stanton Moor and continue forward until reaching the Cork Stone – a large upright stone into which climbing holes have been cut.

☺ This large upright stone is one of several in the area that have been given fanciful names. This one is known as The Cork Stone. Someone in the past cut climbing holes, and at a later date the metal hand grips were added.

5.   At the path fork just beyond the Cork Stone, bear right and continue across the moor to a path crossroads.

Q: What is the dark green, prickly plant that grows amongst the heather on these moors. In summer it has bright yellow flowers.

The Cork Stone, Stanton Moor

A: It is gorse or furze.

6. **Here turn left and follow the path for half a mile to reach The Nine Ladies stone circle.**

☺ As you walk across the moor keep an eye open for meadow pipits. They have a thin, squeaky call.

☺ This Bronze Age circle of stones is known as The Nine Ladies. (English heritage have placed an information plaque beside the stone circle). Legend has it that nine ladies danced here on a Sunday, and as a punishment they were turned into stone. The single stone 30 metres from the circle is supposed to be the fiddler.

7. **From reading the information plaque, turn right and walk towards the stone tower that should be visible through the trees. Cross the stile to examine the tower.**

☺ The tower was built in 1832 to honour Earl Grey, the then Prime Minister, who successfully started the reform of parliamentary voting rights. Before that date parliament was controlled by a small number of privileged people. It is one of many towers to be found around the country which are referred to as "Reform Towers".

8. **Descend the steps in front of the tower, turn right onto the hillside path and follow it around the edge of the moor for approximately three quarters of a mile until reaching a road.**

☺ At the first headland of the moor edge you should find another isolated stone with climbing holes cut into it. This one is known as The Cat Stone. In the valley below (to the south-east), you should see a factory with several slim chimneys. It is built on the site of Millclose Mine which was the largest lead mine in Britain. When the mine closed some of the underground workings extended a mile north to Rowsley.

Q: Which is heavier, a bar of iron or a bar of lead of the same size?
A: The lead bar. It will be nearly half as heavy again as the iron one.

9. **Turn left onto the road to reach a stile in the right-hand hedge 100 metres ahead. Cross this and bear right across grazing land to reach a squeezer stile between a field gate and woodland.**

10. Pass through the stile and, keeping the woodland to your left, advance to another squeezer.

Q: Beside the second squeezer stile there is a large, isolated tree. What type of tree is it?

A: An oak. Can you find any double acorn cups?

11. Pass through the squeezer and follow the enclosed path to a field. Here follow the right-hand boundary to reach a stile beside a field gate.

12. Cross the stile and, keeping a wire fence to your right, continue to and through another squeezer. The path now continues straight forward, passing a tree with a yellow hydrant sign, to join a farm drive.

Q: **(INDICATE THE SIGN ON THE TREE)** What does this yellow sign with a large black 'H' mean?

A: It shows that there is a fire hydrant near the tree. The numbers on the sign state the distance of the hydrant from the tree and its depth in the ground.

13. Follow the drive to the left and when it joins a road (Main Street), turn left, down to your starting point.

Other Places of Interest in the Area

Haddon House, Haddon Road, Bakewell

A complete medieval manor house picturesquely set above the River Wye. It belongs to the Duke of Rutland and has been used as a period setting for numerous films. Telephone 01629 812855 for opening dates and times.

Cauldwell's Mill, Rowsley

A working water-powered flour mill on show. Flour may be purchased during your visit. Telephone 01629 734374 for opening dates and times.

Birchover and Stanton Moor Checklist

- [ ] SILVER BIRCH
- [ ] A GREAT TIT
- [ ] A SYCAMORE
- [ ] QUARRIED STONE
- [ ] AN ACORN
- [ ] IVY-COVERED TREES
- [ ] STONE STEPS
- [ ] NATIONAL TRUST SIGN
- [ ] WAR MEMORIAL
- [ ] A CHAPEL

4. Black Rocks

Black Rocks is the name given to a massive gritstone outcrop located high above Cromford and Wirksworth. Below the rockface there are picnic tables, an information centre and an old lead mine. All is set within the forested slopes of Bole Hill which provides extensive views. Here also is the trackbed of one of the earliest railways, which was built by a canal engineer!

Starting point: The Black Rocks car park (SK291 557). The car park and information centre are 3½ miles south of Matlock. Follow the A6 in the Derby direction to the Cromford junction. Here turn right and follow the A5012 and then B5036 towards Wirksworth. The car park and information centre are signposted to the left, near the road's summit.

By bus: Services from Derby, Bakewell and Matlock

Distance: Entire route 2 miles. Shorter route (using both escape routes) 1 mile.

Terrain: Forest paths and purpose-built track along an old railway trackbed.

Maps: OS Outdoor Leisure Sheet 24

Public Toilets: At the Black Rocks information centre.

Refreshments: None

Pushchairs: Only as a linear walk along an old railway trackbed (High Peak Trail) from the information centre to the Winding House and return. Altogether 1½ miles.

1. Follow the path around the information centre to reach the High Peak Trail. Turn left onto this and within 40 metres you will see an information board to your right.

☺ The ruins beside the information centre are all that remains above ground of the Cromford Moor Mine. Lead was first mined here in 1500 and the shaft descends 120 metres.

Black Rocks

2. **Walk up to the information board, turn right and follow the green and blue-banded marker posts. The path ascends beside the Black Rocks.**
(A careful ascent of the Black Rocks is recommended for the superb view.)

☺ This 25 metre high rock face is known as The Black Rocks. The rocks have been shaped by the action of wind and rain (weathered), and are usually well-used by climbers. The rock is gritstone and consists of millions upon millions of compressed particles of river silt. The rock when first split is golden brown, but soon turns dark brown, almost black, when exposed to the air.

Q: In climbing up towards the Black Rocks you have crossed a scree-type hill. From what do you think this has been formed?

A: It is the spoil heap from the Cromford Moor Mine.

3. **Continue to follow the green and blue-banded marker posts as the path passes behind the Black Rocks and then climbs the side of a disused quarry.**

☺ As you follow the path uphill notice how the trees change. At first you pass through oak and beech trees, which are replaced by silver birch and then conifers and fern-like bracken.

Q: These conifers keep their needles all year. What name is given to trees that shed their needles or leaves?

A: Deciduous.

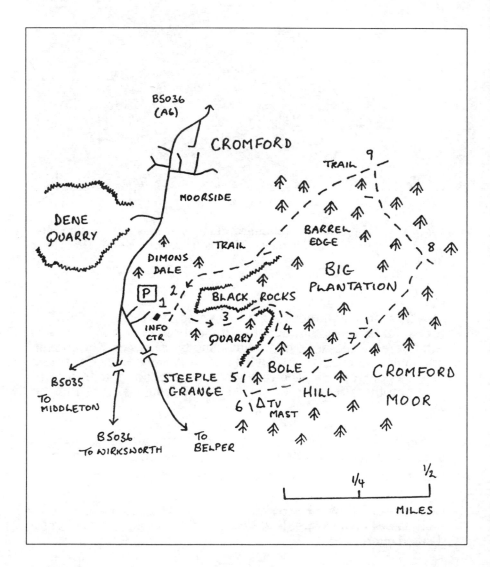

4. **Just after the last set of steps, there is a path junction. Here keep right, following the blue-banded marker posts and a wooden fence, to walk along the rim of a quarry.**
   Escape route: at the aforementioned junction bear left and follow the green-banded marker posts to rejoin the main route at point 7.

☺ To your right is an abandoned quarry, one of many in this area which supplied building stone. **LOOK, BUT DO NOT CROSS THE FENCE.**

5. **At the end of the fence bear left and continue to follow the blue-banded marker posts up to the Ordnance Survey Trig Point on Bole Hill.**

☺ You have now reached the summit of Bole Hill, 1056 feet (322 metres), with its Ordnance Survey pillar and TV transmitter. There is a marvellous view from here. Below you is the town of Wirksworth which has existed for at least 1800 years. From Roman times it has been a lead mining centre but now its main industry is limestone quarrying. As you can see, the town is surrounded by enormous holes in the ground.

6. **With the OS Trig Point and the view behind you, head into the trees again, following the blue-banded marker posts. The path gradually descends for approximately a third of a mile to reach a wall gap.** *(Here the escape route rejoins from the left just before the wall gap – see green-banded marker post.)*

☺ As you walk through this forest you should hear the call of many birds. Can you identify them? Notice that where the light is blocked out, nothing grows on the forest floor and the tree branches are bare. Keep a look out for squirrels and other forest animals such as weasels.

   Escape route: Pass through the gap, turn left and follow the green-banded marker posts to the information board that you passed at the start of your walk.

7. **Pass through the gap and follow the opposing path (blue-banded marker posts) which briefly climbs and then continues the descent through the forest to a path T-junction.**

☺ Notice that the trees, particularly on your left, are packed together. The needles shed by the lack of light have formed a thick carpet on the forest floor.

8. **Turn left and follow the path until it reaches a wall stile at the top of**

a ridge. Do not cross the stile. Follow the path which remains outside the enclosure and descends, via a flight of steps, to the High Peak Trail.

☺ On reaching the wall stile there is a wonderful view of the Derwent Valley. The river itself is virtually hidden as it travels south from Matlock through a narrow gorge. Directly below you in the valley is Cromford Village and its cotton spinning mill. This mill, which was built in 1771, was the first one in the world to be driven by water power.

Q: High above the right-hand side of the valley is Ribber Castle. If you have an Ordnance Survey map, try to find the castle on it. What is the height of the hill on which it is built?

A: 856 feet (261 metres).

(On reaching the High Peak Trail you may wish to detour right for about 40 metres to see the railway gradient which climbs from the Cromford Canal and the remains of the Winding House.)

☺ **(ON REACHING THE HIGH PEAK TRAIL, IDEALLY AT THE TOP OF THE RAILWAY GRADIENT BESIDE THE WINDING HOUSE)** This walking and cycling trail is now known as The High Peak Trail, however, from 1830 to the 1960s, it was the trackbed of the Cromford and High Peak Railway. The railway had to climb very steep hills which were impossible for trains. Wagons had to be pulled up by connecting them to chains or steel cable wound along the tracks by a massive steam engine. The steam engine would have been housed in the large building at the top of the 1:8 gradient.

9.   At the bottom of the steps turn left onto the High Peak Trail and follow this for a mile back to your starting point.

☺ As you walk along the trail, notice how some of the old quarries come right up to the side of the railway trackbed. In places the trackbed had to be cut through the rock and you may see some of the drill holes which held the explosive charge to blast the way forward.

Q: When you reach some massive rocks on your right, look for the carved letters "CHR Co". What do they stand for?

A: "CHR Co" is The Cromford and High Peak Railway Company. Even the railway company wrote graffiti!

Other Places of Interest in the Area

Peak District Mining Museum and Temple Mine, Matlock Bath

Lead mining museum and working, reconstructed lead and fluorspar mine. Mineral panning. Telephone 01629 583834 for opening dates and times.

Black Rocks Checklist

☐ A FIR CONE

☐ HEATHER

☐ A CYCLIST

☐ A ROCK-CLIMBER

☐ TV MAST

☐ A PICNIC TABLE

☐ A SQUIRREL

☐ A RAILWAY WORKER'S SHELTER

5. Blackstone, Birchen and Gordom's Edges

The skyline looking east from the River Derwent, between Ladybower Reservoir and Chatsworth, is dominated by impressive gritstone cliffs or edges. They provide relatively easy high-level walks and panoramic views. The edges are backed by a moorland plateau of heather and bilberry where the solitude is disturbed only by the call of the birds. Blackstone, Birchen and Gordom's Edges overlook Baslow and the northern section of the Chatsworth estate. Two of the edges have the added interest of being surmounted by monuments to the Duke of Wellington and Admiral Lord Nelson.

Starting point: The National Park car park adjacent to the Robin Hood Inn (SK281721). The Robin Hood Inn is 6½ miles west of Chesterfield on the A619.

By bus: Services from Chesterfield and Bakewell

Distance: Entire route 4¾ miles. Shorter route 3½ miles.

Terrain: Mostly moorland paths and tracks. A little rock scrambling in the first mile, but nothing beyond the capability of most children. Can be boggy as you approach points 7 and 13.

Maps: OS Outdoor Leisure Sheet 24

Public Toilets: None, but the ones at the Robin Hood Inn may be used by customers.

Refreshments: Robin Hood Inn

Pushchairs: Unsuitable

1. Return to the car park entrance, turn left and follow the road past a house. Just after the house bear left and follow a short track up to a field gate. Cross the stile near the gate and enter the National Park's East Moor Estate.

2. Follow the sand and rock path uphill, keeping the garden wall to

your left. **The garden is succeeded by a mini golf course and then a field, before it turns away, left, from your path.**

Q: (AT THE MINI GOLF COURSE) How many "putting greens" does this mini golf course have?

A: 9

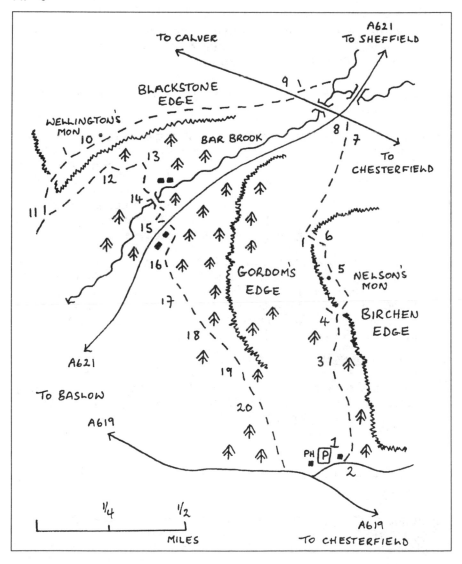

☺ Notice how sandy the soil is here. The action of wind and rain grinds away the surface of the rocks to leave sand or fine grit. The rocks are made of gritstone which was formed 230 million years ago from particles of silt. This was deposited by a great river which here met a sea that then covered what is now southern Britain.

Q: Do you know the name of the trees that are around you?

A: They are silver birches. They take their name from the colour of their bark. Notice how shallow their roots are and that they spread out along the ground like fingers.

3. **Continue forward, ignoring all minor paths, until you near the rock face of Birchen Edge.**

☺ This rock face is known as Birchen Edge and at weekends it is a magnet for rock-climbers. It is great entertainment to watch them climb — they look like ants! This gritstone is ideal for rock-climbing with its rough surface.

4. **Take the path that leads away right from the main undercliff path to the base of the rock face. Here you should find an easy scrambling route to the top. After which, turn left to reach Nelson's Monument.**

☺ The stone pillar at the top of the rock face is known as Nelson's Monument or Pole. It was erected in memory of Admiral Lord Nelson (1758 – 1805) and the Battle of Trafalgar in which he died. Behind the monument there are three large rocks on which the names of the most famous British ships in that battle are carved. Notice that *Sovereign* is spelt incorrectly.

5. **Continue along the edge to the trig point.**

☺ This white pillar is known as a trig, or triangulation point. Trig points were set up by the Ordnance Survey after 1845 on numerous sites in Britain to enable them to survey the country and hence produce maps. Today trig points are no longer used, as aerial and satellite photography provide far more accurate mapping details. On the OS Map can you find the trig points that surround Birchen Edge? They are indicated by a small blue triangle.

☺ Notice that very little else apart from purple-flowering heather grows on this plateau. Amongst the heather you may catch a glimpse of red grouse. Their food is the heather's new growth.

The Three Ships, Birchen Edge

Very often there are sheep grazing right up to the edge – they must have a wonderful sense of balance.

6. **Immediately after the trig point, descend the edge via a gully path to meet a well-defined path. Turn right onto the path and follow it directly north, through heather and birch and then over marsh land, to a ladder stile near a crossroads.**

☺ As you walk away from Birchen Edge the ground becomes damp. Notice how the types of plants and trees change as the presence of water increases. Heather virtually disappears, as do the silver birch trees. Sedge grasses and rushes take their place.

7. **Cross the stile and turn left to the crossroads (A621 and B6050). TAKE CARE AS THIS CAN BE A BUSY ROAD JUNCTION**
   Escape route: At the crossroads turn left and follow the pavement until you meet the main route at point 15, opposite Cupola Cottage.

8. **Continue straight ahead at the crossroads, over the Bar Brook, and climb with the road to reach a gate on your left.**

☺ **(AT THE BRIDGE)** The Bar Brook, immediately downstream of the bridge, is often home to Longhorn cattle. Hopefully they are there when you visit this spot. They make a wonderful sight with their long, rusty-coloured hair and massive horns

(Before turning left through the gate, you may wish to cross the stile opposite and follow the bridle path down to the old clapper bridge.)

☺ This is the old crossing of the Bar Brook. The bridge consists of two massive stones and is therefore known as a clapper bridge. On one of the stones is carved the date 1742.

9. **Turn left through the gate and follow the well-defined track along the edge to Wellington's Monument**

☺ Just after leaving the road you will see a stone pillar on your left. This is a guide stone and on one face has the inscription "Chesterfeild Roade". These stones were erected at junctions from 1702. It has been moved from its former position as the bridle road junction was further east of here. Notice that only one destination is shown!

Q: What is wrong with the spelling of the town?

A: The " i " and "e " in Chesterfield have been reversed.

☺ **(AT THE MONUMENT)** This cross is known as Wellington's Monument. It was erected in 1866 in memory of the Duke of Wellington (1769 − 1852), of wellington boot fame, and his victories, particularly the Battle of Waterloo. From here you should see Nelson's Monument on Birchen Edge (south-east) with Gordom's Edge below it.

☺ On the moor behind the monument is a large rock known as the Eagle Rock. It is believed that the word "eagle" is derived from "Aigle", a pagan god who apparently could project large rocks through the air.

10. **Follow the path that descends towards Baslow and passes through an old quarry to a gate, beside which is an Access Land sign.**

11. **Immediately before the gate turn sharp left and follow the path which clings to the right-hand side of a field wall. The wall in places is broken and replaced by a wire fence. Bracken overgrows the path here and a little effort is needed to press forward.**

12. **When you are directly below Wellington's Monument, the wall/fence that you have been following drops away to your right. Here continue forward through rock-strewn woodland until the wall reappears on your right.**

Q: What type of tree is mainly to be found in these woods?

A: Oak. They are very old. Notice how their trunks and branches have twisted in various directions. In these woods there are various types of fungi — **DO NOT TOUCH OR EAT THEM**. On the rocks notice the different types of lichen, which in places are red in colour. Lichen indicates clean air.

13. Now follow the path, which keeps fairly close to the right-hand side of the wall down to a stile.

14. Cross the stile and follow the path which now runs along the edge of a garden and down to a bridge. Cross this and follow the path to the A621 (Sheffield to Baslow road).

☺ **(AT THE BRIDGE)** This is an old packhorse bridge. The water makes a wonderful sound as it tumbles over rocks in this pretty, wooded gorge. You should see many birds in this area, particularly the wren-shaped dippers with their dark plumage and white chests. They sit on the rocks curtseying before entering the water.

15. Cross the road to a couple of wall steps to the left of Cupola Cottage *(the escape route rejoins here).* Once over these continue ahead to a stile. Cross this and bear right to follow the left-hand side of the wire fence boundary of Cupola Cottage and Toll Bar House.

16. When the wire fence turns sharply away to the right, you should continue along the path which bears left and rises gently to meet the corner of a wall.

☺ Notice here that there are both silver and brown birch trees. In the more open areas you may see birds such as the rare ring ouzel which looks like a blackbird but has a grey tinge and a white flash on its chest.

17. Again the path is clearly defined as it steadily climbs away from the wall, passes through a wall gap and shortly enters rock-strewn, oak woodland.

☺ **(IN THE WOODS)** These rocks have been broken away from the cliffs above by the action of ice. The cliffs are known as Gordom's Edge and are believed to be named after the owner of the cotton mill at Calver.

18. Pass through the woods and cross a sunken path to reach a wall gap.

☺ Just after the rock-strewn area, notice the sunken path that crosses your path. This has been worn by people climbing up to gather firewood in times past.

19. **Pass through the gap and continue up across open ground to another gap. Once through this make your way to the top of the rocks on your left.**

☺ What interesting shapes these rocks have. They look like a group of fat-bellied jars. From their summit you should have a wonderful view.

20. **Now return to the path which follows the edge of the plateau and turn left to follow it down to a stile on the A619 (Baslow to Chesterfield road).**

21. **Cross the stile, turn left and follow the pavement back to the Robin Hood Inn.**

Blackstone, Birchen and Gordom's Edges Checklist

☐ AN ARCHER

☐ A STONE BALL

☐ A GROUSE

☐ HEATHER

☐ FUNGI

☐ A FLAG POLE

☐ A ROCK-CLIMBER

☐ LONGHORN CATTLE

☐ A WATER TROUGH

☐ A SYCAMORE TREE *(WITH BLACK-SPOTTED LEAVES)*

6. Calke Abbey Park and Ticknall

Calke Abbey is the name given to the mansion built for the Harpur family in a 300 hectare park and on the site of an Augustinian Abbey. This walk takes you through the park's ancient oak woods and around its fish lakes. It also passes through Ticknall village which once had thriving lime, pottery and brick-making industries. The lime kilns and the remains of a very old railway can be seen.

Starting point: The car park adjacent to Calke Abbey (SK366 227). Calke Abbey is 11 miles south of Derby and is clearly signposted from the A514 in Ticknall village. Calke Abbey and its park are owned by the National Trust. The park is open throughout the year, but access other than via the rights of way can only be obtained during daylight hours. There is a parking charge.

By bus: Services from Derby to the park entrance in Ticknall. Start from point 9.

Distance: Entire route 3 miles

Terrain: Mostly parkland footpaths and tracks. Short section across arable/grazing land and a little pavement walking. Level throughout except for the gentle slopes around the park's lake area.

Maps: OS Landranger 128 and Pathfinder 852

Public Toilets: None, but there are toilets in the Calke Abbey restaurant courtyard.

Refreshments: Calke Abbey restaurant and the Staff of Life pub, Ticknall

Pushchairs: Unsuitable

1. **Make your way into the overspill section of the car park and walk up to the deer fence.**

☺ **(INDICATE THE DEER ENCLOSURE)** This part of the park has been reserved for deer grazing. Deer are very timid and will run away from noise, sudden movement or the scent of people. If you are lucky, they will venture close enough for your inspection.

Q: What are male deer called?

A: Stags. They have horns which are called antlers. These are shed annually and grow back even longer in the following year.

2. **Now make your way towards the corner formed by the fencing and the line of horse chestnut trees. About 30 metres left of the corner, in amongst the trees, you should find a rough path. Follow this down to the lake.**

Q: On leaving the car park you pass under some horse chestnut trees. What is the seed of these trees called?

A: A conker.

3. **On reaching the lake turn right and follow the perimeter path to the lake's outflow.**

Calke Abbey

🙂 This lake has many fish which you may see as they swim in the shallows or near the surface. The large fish will probably be carp, which can live for 40 years and grow to 40 centimetres, but there are other species here including tench. Can you spot the fisherman's competitor — the heron?

4. **Here pass through a gate and climb away from the lake. Keep the deer fencing directly to your right until you reach the edge of the woods.**

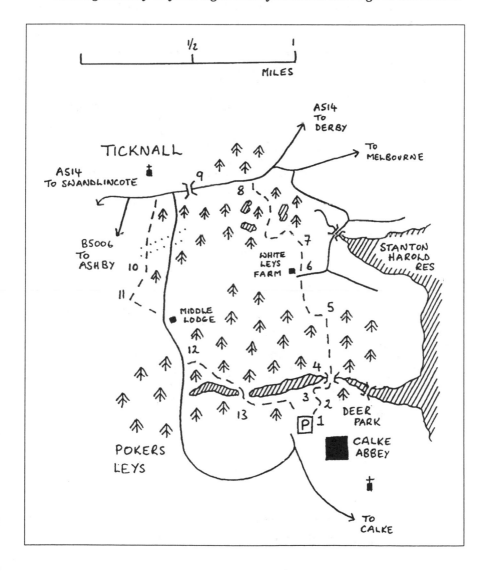

☺ The oak trees through which you are passing are probably some 300 years old. You may think that this is old but later you will see some that make these seem like youngsters!

☺ During the summer the ground under the trees is covered with bracken, a non-flowering fern-like plant. Animals will not eat this plant as it is poisonous to them.

5. Turn left on to the woodland perimeter path and after about 40 metres you will see a gate to your right. Pass through this and immediately turn left to a stile. Cross this and head diagonally right across the field, aiming for a stile to the right of White Leys Farm.

☺ To your right there are views of Staunton Harold Reservoir with its picnic areas and nature reserve. *(See "Other Places of Interest in the Area".)* Part of the reservoir — that to your far right — lies in Leicestershire.

6. Cross the farm track, pass along the right-hand (eastern) side of the farm and then continue forward, keeping an overgrown wall to your left. (Ignore the path that departs to the right by a large, isolated ash tree.)

☺ The farmer usually plants crops in these fields. Can you identify what has been planted?

7. At the end of the wall, continue straight ahead through a field entrance to follow the left-hand side of a hedge towards woodland. On reaching the woodland perimeter track, turn left and follow it into and through the woods. On the far side of the woods the track passes some cottages on the outskirts of Ticknall village, and meets the A514 (Derby to Swadlincote road).

☺ The lakes in these woods fill pits which were dug to obtain limestone for the production of lime. They now contain pike, perch, carp and many other kinds of fish. Around the lakes there are old lime kilns. Limestone was packed into these and heated to more than 800 degrees centigrade to form lime. The lime would be used by builders to make mortar and plaster. Clay was also dug in this area to produce bricks and pottery.

☺ As you pass along the woodland track you can see that many of the trees are covered with creepers. These are clematis plants called "Traveller's Joy" and they give the impression that the trees have thousands of aerial roots.

8. Turn left on to the A514 and follow it to a bridge.

☺ **(INDICATE THE PUMP AT THE ROADSIDE, ON YOUR LEFT AFTER DERBY HOUSE)** This is one of the village's old pumps. Before water was piped to the village houses, the people had to collect all of their water from these. Can you imagine collecting and carrying the water used in your home from such a street pump!

☺ **(A LITTLE FURTHER ON AND TO YOUR RIGHT, INDICATE THE STY)** If you look over the wall to your right you will see a pig-sty. It is now very rare to see a sty such as this in a village. Pigs love to lie in the mud, but their smell is not so lovely!

☺ The bridge under which you now pass was built around 1800 to carry a narrow gauge railway. The railway used to transport lime from the village kilns.

9. Pass under the bridge and just after the road entrance to Calke Abbey, turn left over a stile. Now follow the path, keeping a house, its garden and then a wood to your left, to reach another stile. Cross this and continue along the edge of the woods to pass through a chicane formed from wooden fences.

☺ **(INDICATE THE TUNNEL ENTERANCE IMMEDIATELY BELOW AND TO YOUR RIGHT)** This 130 metre tunnel was used by the lime railway to travel under the driveway of Calke Abbey. You can see the old bed of the railway as it leaves this end of the tunnel and runs between the trees. The line used to run to Ashby de la Zouch, four miles away in Leicestershire, where it joined the mainline railway and a canal.

10. Continue ahead and cross the stile into Calke Abbey park. Bear right and follow the clear path until you reach a stile on your right.

11. Here turn diagonally left, cutting across the grassland to Middle Lodge. Pass through the pedestrian gate (there is free pedestrian entrance to the park during daylight hours), and follow the drive until it bends right just after passing through some oak trees.

☺ Lodges were the homes of gatekeepers. Some can be very small houses and have odd shapes.

12. The drive is joined on the left by a gated track. Turn left onto this and just after the gate proceed diagonally right to follow a path through the oak trees. Shortly you will emerge above a lake and the path then runs diagonally down to its outfall.

☺ **(POINT OUT THE ANCIENT OAK TREES)** These old and

gnarled oak trees were here well before the present Calke Abbey was built in 1703. They are from medieval times, as are those which are to be seen in Sherwood Forest.

13. **After passing the end of the lake, cross a stile and climb the steps to a path that runs above the bank of another lake. On reaching a further stile turn right and climb back up to your starting point.**

Other Places of Interest in the Area

Calke Abbey, Gardens and Church

The mansion built in 1703 for Sir John Harpur. The interior is a Victorian time capsule as Sir Vauncey Harpur-Crew (1846-1924) and his family endeavoured not to let the 20th century into the estate. Telephone 01332 863822 for opening dates and times.

Staunton Harold Reservoir, Melbourne

A 90 hectare reservoir with sailing, fishing, bird-watching, nature reserve and picnic areas. Visitor centre and a converted mill which acts as an observation point. Telephone 01332 865081 for opening dates and times.

Calke Abbey Checklist

- [ ] SHEEP
- [ ] A CATTLE GRID
- [ ] DEER
- [ ] A PIG
- [ ] AN ASH TREE
- [ ] A HOLLY BUSH
- [ ] A HERON
- [ ] A FISH
- [ ] WATER LILIES
- [ ] A WATER PUMP

7. *Carsington Water*

Derbyshire has no natural lakes. Those that do exist are reservoirs and the latest addition is the one known as Carsington Water, located between Ashbourne and Wirksworth. The route along part of the reservoir's western shore is virtually flat and uses well maintained all-weather surfaces. It provides one of the best opportunities to observe, particularly from free access hides, the diverse and prolific wildfowl which live on or visit the reservoir.

Starting point: The visitor centre car park, Carsington Water (SK241 516). The visitor centre is 5 miles north-west of Ashbourne. Take the B5035 towards Wirksworth and after approximately 4½ miles, at Knockerdown, the reservoir is signposted to your right. There is a parking charge.

By bus: Limited services from Ashbourne and Matlock

Distance: Entire route 2½ miles

Terrain: Purpose-built all-weather tracks and a short section of minor road walking. Virtually flat throughout.

Maps: OS Outdoor Leisure Sheet 24

Public Toilets: At the Visitor Centre

Refreshments: Café/restaurant at the Visitor Centre

Pushchairs: Totally suitable

☺ Carsington Water reservoir was opened by Her Majesty Queen Elizabeth II in 1992. It was formed by damming the Scow Brook and can hold up to 36 billion litres of water. Water can be pumped to or from the reservoir via an underground pipeline which runs 6 miles west to a pump house on the banks of the River Derwent near Whatstandwell. When the Derwent contains more water than is required by consumers and its own ecological needs, the excess is diverted to Carsington Water for storage. However, when the Derwent cannot meet the demand for water, the flow in

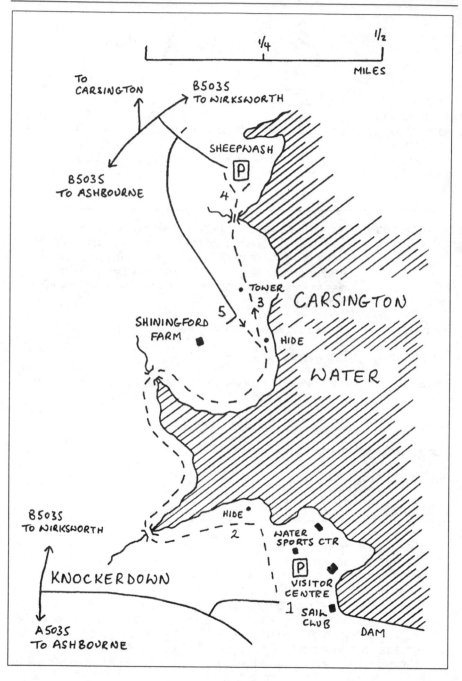

the pipe is reversed. Water leaves and enters the reservoir via the tall, cylindrical building which is located in the water near the far (Millfields) end of the dam.

(The Visitors Centre has a hands-on exhibition, ideal for children and adults alike, showing how the reservoir was built and its operation. There is also a wildfowl observation point with a remote control camera. The Water Sports Centre hires cycles and water sports equipment.)

1. **Return to the visitor centre car park's approach road. A few yards into this you will see a crossing bridle path. Here turn right and follow the path which is waymarked "CW5" along the western edge of the parking area.**

☺ **(POINT OUT THE SMALL, TWO STOREY BUILDING IN THE CAR PARK)** This small building used to be a nonconformist chapel. At one time nonconformists were not allowed to worship inside a settlement containing a Church of England church or chapel. Hence this chapel's location amongst the fields and about one mile from Hognagston parish church. The building has been rebuilt as it was mistakenly demolished during the construction of the reservoir. It now serves as the headquarters of the Carsington Water ranger service.

2. **Continue along the path when it departs from the car park, to pass a bird- watching hide and reach the western edge of the reservoir. Follow the yellow- painted posts along the bank (the blue ones denote the route for horses and cyclists) for approximately 1 mile, to a second hide.**

☺ Along the water's edge there are hides which, provided that you are very quiet, should allow you to observe the many species of birds that live on or just visit the reservoir and its reed beds. You should spot great crested greeb (these are the ones with a halo of neck feathers), mallard and tufted ducks, geese, moorhens (which are dark brown/black with red beaks), coot (which are black with white beaks), kingfisher and many others.

3. **Continue to follow the yellow posts past an old watch tower (left), and in approximately a quarter of a mile cross a bridge to reach Sheepwash car park.**

☺ **(POINT OUT THE TOWER)** This used to be a watchtower during World War II. With the hides it now provides a very good point from which to observe the reservoir's bird life.

☺ Many years ago the streams near the Sheepwash car park were

Mallards queuing for a drink at Carsington Water

dammed each year at sheep-shearing time. The pools formed were used to wash the sheep so that the fleeces would be relatively clean before being sold.

4. **Here turn left and follow the road to the entrance gates. Pass through these gates and then turn sharply left, following the lane past the entrance to Shinning Ford Farm and back to the second hide.**

☺ When the Romans occupied Britain they constructed a wooden building in the valley that has now been flooded to form Carsington Water. In the building they processed the lead mined in the limestone hills just north of the reservoir. At the end of the process lead was poured into moulds and allowed to cool. The resultant ingot of lead was and still is known as a "Pig of Lead". A Roman ingot was found in the fields hereabouts.

5. **From here return to the visitor centre car park by retracing your outward journey.**

Other Places of Interest In The Area

National Stone Centre, Porter Lane, Wirksworth

Exhibition and displays telling the story of stone from when it was formed to the present day. Includes the stone quarry industry and its products. There is a limestone quarry fossil trail and gem panning. Telephone 01629 824833 and 825403 for opening dates and times.

Carsington Water Checklist

☐ A SAILBOAT

☐ A BICYCLE

☐ A FISHERMAN

☐ A TOWER

☐ AN ISLAND

☐ A WINDSURFER

☐ A PUMP TOWER

8. Chatsworth Park

Chatsworth Park, which extends to over 450 hectares on both banks of the River Derwent, is open to the public almost in its entirety. Follow the river through parkland where red and fallow deer can be observed, past the park's magnificent centre piece, Chatsworth House, or walk through woods with secluded lakes, to return across the moors.

Starting point: Carlton Lees car park at the southern end of Chatsworth Park (SK259 686). The car park is 5 miles west of Bakewell. Take the A6 towards Matlock and at Rowsley turn on to the B6012. The car park is signposted just after Beeley (One Arch) Bridge.

By bus: Services from Matlock and Baslow (except Sundays).

Distance: Entire route 4½ miles

Terrain: Mostly estate paths and tracks. Virtually level from the car park to Chatsworth House and along the ridge above the park. There is a long and steep flight of steps up to the Hunting Tower but it is well worth the effort. The concessionary path between points 3 and 5 can be closed during events which are being held in the park. It may be worth checking with the Chatsworth Estate Office (telephone 01246 582204) before you visit.

Maps: OS Outdoor Leisure Sheet 24

Public Toilets: In the Carlton Lees car park, near the entrance to the garden centre. Also in the Garden Centre and outside Chatsworth House and its restaurant.

Refreshments: Chatsworth House Restaurant, café in the Garden Centre and a kiosk in the Carlton Lees car park.

Pushchairs: Unsuitable

1. **Return to the car park entrance and walk up to the white gates on the B6012 (Rowsley to Baslow road). Pass through the pedestrian gate, cross the road and descend to the riverbank near a ruined mill.**

☺ **(OUTSIDE THE RUINED MILL)** This building used to be a corn mill powered by a waterwheel. It was built in 1757 and last ground corn in 1952. Unfortunately, the building was extensively damaged during the gales of 1967 when a huge beech tree fell on top of it.

2. **Turn left and follow the path upstream until you reach Chatsworth Bridge.**

☺ **(AT THE RIVER BANK)** This is the River Derwent. It is one of Britain's finest trout fishing rivers, and as you pass along the river bank you may see fishermen standing in the water using "flies" to catch trout. On warm days it is nice to paddle in the shallows below the first weir.

☺ The land on the other side of the river is known as the Old Park and is often grazed by red and fallow deer (the fallow deer look like Bambi). Can you see any?

Q: What is a female deer called?

A: A doe or hind.

☺ Sometimes there are deer on this side of the river, but usually you will find sheep grazing here. Amongst the flocks you may see Jacob's sheep – the ones with brown-spotted fleeces. They gained their name from the Bible and it is believed that they came form the Holy Land via North Africa and Spain.

3. **Cross the bridge and take the right-hand path through a gate (start of the concessionary path) and up to the main entrance to Chatsworth House.**

☺ The building on your left is known as Queen Mary's Bower. This raised and walled garden was a favourite haunt of Mary, Queen of Scots when she was imprisoned at Chatsworth in the 16th century. Her coat of arms can be seen over the gateway. The moat is one of the fish ponds belonging to the original Chatsworth House.

☺ To your right is Chatsworth House, the home of the Duke and Duchess of Devonshire. It was built between 1687 and 1707 to replace the 16th-century house built by the Countess of

Shrewsbury. Chatsworth is commonly referred to as the "The Palace of the Peak". You may notice that the window frames on the west front glow when the sun catches them. This is because they are edged in gold leaf.

Chatsworth House

4. **Now follow the road up and round the left-hand side of the car park to a cattle grid. Pass around this and when the road splits three ways, take the middle course which starts to climb up through the woods.** *(The road to the left leads to the children's farmyard and adventure playground – see "Other Places of Interest in the Area.)*

☺ The wood covering the hillside behind Chatsworth House and through which you now climb, is known as Stand Wood. Stand means a place of height for spectators, hence "grandstand" at a sports arena. The wood was originally planted during the period 1750-1850 with beech, sycamore, chestnut and conifers, but many other species have been added since that time. Oak from here was given to the restoration of York Minster following its damage by fire in 1984. This wood abounds with many species of birds. See how many you can spot.

5. **Now either follow the main estate road all the way up to the Hunting Tower or take the footpath on your left. The path crosses an estate road and then reaches a long flight of steps leading to the Hunting Tower – WARNING: THESE STEPS CAN BE HAZARDOUS IN WET OR ICY CONDITIONS.**

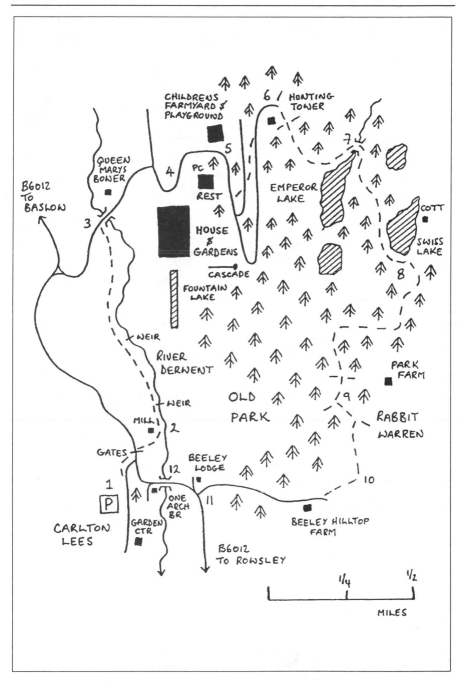

CHILDRENS
FARMYARD &
PLAYGROUND

6 / HUNTING
TOWER

5

QUEEN
MARYS
BOWER

4

PC

REST

B6012
TO
BASLOW

3

HOUSE
&
GARDENS

EMPEROR
LAKE

7

COTT

SWISS
LAKE

CASCADE

8

FOUNTAIN
LAKE

WEIR

RIVER
DERWENT

PARK
FARM

WEIR

OLD
PARK

MILL

2

9

RABBIT
WARREN

GATES

BEELEY
LODGE

12

10

1

P

ONE
ARCH
BR

11

CARLTON
LEES

GARDEN
CTR

BEELEY HILLTOP
FARM

B6012
TO ROWSLEY

1/4   1/2

MILES

☺ The building in front of you is known as The Hunting Tower. It was previously called Stand Tower and was built in 1582 in order to watch the hounds hunting in the valley below. The cannon at the base of the tower came from a ship that fought at the Battle of Trafalgar.

6. Follow the road around the tower and ignore the track on the left signposted "Robin Hood". Also ignore the next left and the track that enters on your right from the other side of the tower. At the next junction take the left-hand track and follow this to the Emperor Lake.

☺ This is the Emperor Lake which collects water from the moors east of Chatsworth House and feeds the Emperor Fountain in Chatsworth House Gardens. The fountain has a single jet which rises to 81 metres. The water also drives a turbine which provides electricity to the house. Look out for water voles along the edges of the lake and in the surrounding wetlands.

7. Continue along the track – it crosses the Emperor Stream and shortly reaches the Swiss Lake.

☺ This lake is another reservoir and feeds the Cascade in Chatsworth House Gardens. The cottage and the lake gained the title "Swiss" after the 6th Duke returned from a visit to Switzerland in1839.

8. Continue along the track, ignoring all side paths. When a crossroads is reached (the left turn leads to Park Farm), continue straight ahead, but at the next junction turn left and head for a wall stile at the park boundary.

☺ As you pass through the woodland, keep an eye out for squirrels, weasels and, if you are lucky, foxes, too.

9. Cross the stile and follow the track which runs along the top edge of the moorland hillside. Just before the track leaves the drystone wall, turn diagonally right and follow a path down to a very high wall stile beside a locked door.

☺ This hillside is usually covered with a non-flowering fern-like plant, bracken. In the autumn the bracken turns brown and is a wonderful sight. This entire hillside is covered with rabbit holes (burrows) and is known as a warren.

10. Climb over the wall and head across the field towards Beeley Hilltop Farm. In the corner of the field nearest to the farm there is a stile (the

concessionary path ends here). Cross this, turn right and follow the
path down to the B6012 (Rowsley to Baslow road).

☺ **(AFTER THE ROAD EMERGES FROM THE WOODS INDICATE
THE PARKLAND TO YOUR RIGHT)** The parkland on your right
is the Old Park that you saw earlier from the riverbank. You now
have another chance to see the deer. You should also see some
ancient, gnarled oak trees.

11. Here turn right and follow the road past Blue Doors Lodge to One
    Arch Bridge.

☺ This is Blue Doors Lodge which guards the southern, private and
now seldom used entrance to Chatsworth Park. When the railway
reached Rowsley, 1½ miles south of here, in 1849, this was the
main entrance for visitors. They came by horse-drawn buses and
on foot from the station – 80,000 in that year.

☺ **(AT THE BRIDGE)** This is One Arch Bridge which was built in
1757. Below the bridge the arch has been closed by netting. This
is to stop the deer swimming out of the park – oh yes, they are
good swimmers!

12. Cross the bridge and as the road climbs away to the right, leave it
    and climb the bank back to Carlton Lees car park.

☺ Often pheasants stroll among the cars. Watch out for the ducks.
They patrol the car park and sometimes they can be heard
tapping their bills on the side of the cars demanding to be fed. If
they are not given part of your picnic they stage a sit-in so that
you are unable to move your car.

Other Places of Interest in the Area

Chatsworth House and Gardens

A palatial house built for William Cavendish between 1687 and 1707,
with 19th century additions. The home of the Duke and Duchess of
Devonshire. The garden of some 40 hectares was laid out by Capability
Brown with wonderful water features. Telephone 01246 582204 for
opening dates and times.

The Children's Farmyard and Adventure Playground, Chatsworth Park

The farm provides a living exhibition of pigs, hens, cows, sheep, horses and fish farming with occasional demonstrations. Telephone 01246 582204 for opening dates and times.

Chatsworth Park Checklist

☐ A STATUE

☐ A CATTLE-GRID

☐ AN OAK TREE

☐ A SQUIRREL

☐ A STAG

☐ A CHURCH SPIRE

☐ A WEIR

☐ RHODODENDRONS

☐ A CANNON

☐ JACOB'S SHEEP

9. Cromford Canal

This canal has long since ceased to be a means of transport, but it leaves many reminders of its working days. One of its customers was the great cotton mill at Cromford which could claim to be the birthplace of the Industrial Revolution. The deep-sided Derwent Valley, in which the canal is set, was always beautiful and nature has been kind in its reclamation of man's work. The route follows the initial stage of the canal and also visits one of the first railway sites in the world. Here there is interest at every turn whether it be nature, industrial heritage or scenery.

Starting point: Cromford Wharf pay and display car park (SK300 570). The car park is 2½ miles south of Matlock. Follow the A6 to the Cromford junction, turn left onto Mill Road and the car park is signposted to your right after 400 metres.

By bus: Services from Matlock and Alfreton (no winter Sunday service). Also from Matlock, Derby, Bakewell, Buxton and Manchester to the A6 Cromford road junction – walk down Mill Road for 400 metres.

By train: Service from Matlock and Derby to Cromford Station. 400 metre walk – follow the riverbank road south-westwards and then cross Cromford Bridge.

Distance: Entire route 3½ miles

Terrain: Towpaths, a purpose-made walking trail along the trackbed of an old railway (part of this has a 1:8 gradient), and pavement beside a quiet, residential road.

Maps: OS Outdoor Leisure Sheet 24

Public Toilets: In the Cromford Wharf car park and at the High Peak Junction information centre.

Refreshments: Café at Cromford Mill

Pushchairs: Suitable throughout although a little effort is required whilst climbing the old railway gradient of 1:8.

1. **From the car park, walk up to the towpath. Turn left and continue along the canal for approximately 1¼ miles, to reach a swing-bridge at High Peak Junction.**

☺ This is the Cromford Canal which opened in 1794 to provide for the cheap and reliable transport of bulk goods such as cotton, coal, lead and stone. In those days there was no railway here and the roads were in poor condition — only able to take wheeled carts. The canal connected with other waterways and gave access to Nottingham, Derby, Manchester and Liverpool.

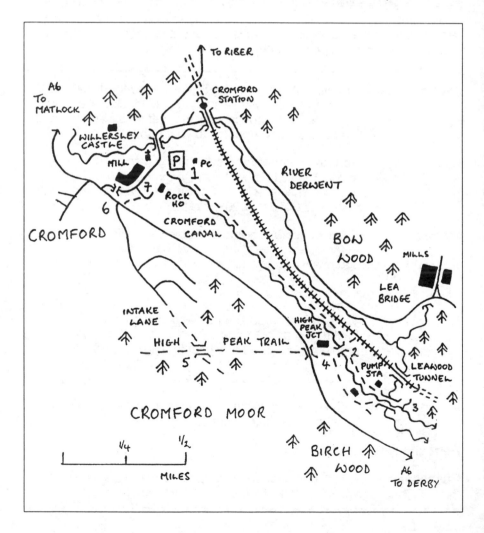

One of the main users of the canal was Cromford Mill (see "Other Places of Interest in the Area"), located across the road from the canal wharf. This was the first cotton spinning mill in the world to use water power. Cotton fibres would have arrived at this canal wharf from the southern states of the USA.

The canal wharf is home to many ducks and other waterfowl. They gather here as your picnic spot is usually theirs as well! You may wish to save a little of your picnic to feed them when you return here.

Q: The path that you are about to follow along the canal is known as a "towpath". Why is it so called?

A: Before canal boats or barges were motorised, they had to be towed (pulled) by a rope attached to a horse while it walked along the path. Notice the rope marks on the sides of the first bridge that you come to.

☺ Further down the canal and on your right, you should see a factory with large overhead cranes. This is a marble works. Stone is here cut and polished, a process requiring constant cooling with water. Unfortunately, the waste water runs into the canal and turns it white for some distance.

2. **On reaching the swing-bridge, continue along the towpath to another at the far end of an aqueduct.**

☺ The canal around this swing-bridge is often home to mute swans and little grebe. The grebe, with its burgundy-coloured face and neck, looks like a puff ball of feathers.

☺ The building with the tall chimney to the left of the towpath is Leawood Pump House. It was built in 1849 to pump water from the River Derwent and replenish the canal if it could not maintain its water level. The huge steam engine inside the building is able to raise 5 tonnes of water per minute from the river 10 metres below the canal. (Demonstrations are given on some summer weekends — see High Peak Junction information centre for details.)

Q: Just after the pump house you will come to a bridge which carries the canal over the river. What name is given to such a bridge?

A: It is called an aqueduct. Within a few months of its completion in 1793 this one started to crack and had to be rebuilt.

☺ The aqueduct provides an ideal point from which to observe the many birds to be found in this area. You may see woodpeckers, grey wagtails with their yellow undercarriage and long tails, kingfishers, finches and many others.

(At the end of the aqueduct a brief detour to your left is recommended. Follow the path alongside the now foreshortened Leawood Branch or Nightingale Arm of the canal (do not cross it) for some 100 metres, to reach a footbridge at the mouth of Leawood Tunnel. Return by the same route.)

☺ The canal branch at the end of the aqueduct used to serve the textile mill at Lea Bridge some 700 metres north of here. The mills were owned by the Nightingale family of whom Florence, "The Lady of The Lamp", is the famous member. She was born, and for many years lived, at Lea Hurst. The woods on the far side of the canal branch are known as Leawood and lead up to the house. How different the Crimea (Ukraine) and its war must have been to Derbyshire!

☺ The footbridge marks the spot where the canal and its towpath used to cross the railway. The railway was the mainline from London to Manchester via Derby, but sadly it is now reduced to a single track which runs between Derby and Matlock.

Q: How long is Leawood Tunnel?
A: 315 yards.

3. **Cross the swing-bridge, turn right and recross the aqueduct. In less than 100 metres the canalside path meets the trackbed of an old railway. Here turn right and follow the track to the High Peak Junction information centre.**

☺ The first buildings on your right are old warehouses and they mark the location of High Peak Wharf. The path that you are following used to be a railway and this is the point where goods were transferred between the canal barges and the railway wagons. Notice the base of an old crane and the loading gauge hanging over the old railway trackbed. Goods were never allowed to be stacked on the wagons above the height of this gauge which equals the clearance of the lowest bridge or tunnel on the railway.

Cromford Junction Railway Workshops

☺ It was originally planned to continue the canal to Whaley Bridge – 10 miles south-east of Stockport – where it would join the High Peak Canal, giving direct access to Manchester. However, the Peak District hills proved too high to be crossed by a canal and the link was provided via a railway. That railway started here and was called The Cromford and High Peak Railway. It opened in 1831 and was one of the first railways to operate anywhere in the world. The information centre's buildings were the railway's workshops.

4.   **From the information centre, walk up the old railway incline for approximately two thirds of a mile to where a footpath is signposted to your left.**

☺ Many of the inclines on the railway were too steep for trains. Wagons had to be pulled up and let down by attaching them to chains or steel wires which were wound along the tracks by huge steam engines built at the top of each incline. The incline that you are now climbing has a gradient of 1:8. It lasts for approximately 1.3 kms and rises 160 metres, that is a rise of 1 metre for every 8 metres travelled.

Q: Just after the A6 road bridge there is a pit which would have been located between the up and down tracks. What do you think it was for?

A: It was built to catch runaway wagons!

5. **Turn left and follow the short footpath down to Intake Lane. Turn left onto the lane and follow it for approximately two thirds of a mile down to the A6 trunk road.**

Q: On the footpath signpost beside the railway trackbed there are some numbers. What are they and what do they mean?

A: 304 562. They are the Grid Reference for this spot and allow you to find it on the Ordnance Survey map. OS maps explain how to use a Grid Reference. If you have such a map see if you can locate your position using the Grid Reference.

☺ The lane which you follow down the hillside is called Intake Lane. It describes the narrow, enclosed way by which crops and animals were moved from the fields into the village.

6. **Cross the A6 to a gap in the opposing wall and follow the subsequent footpath down to the drive of Rock House. Here turn left to reach Mill Road.**

☺ **(AT THE POINT THAT ROCK HOUSE DRIVE MEETS MILL ROAD)** In front of you are the fortress-like outer walls of Cromford Cotton Mill. Cotton mills were built in this way to withstand attacks by people intent on wrecking the mill's machinery. They were angry at the loss of jobs to machines.

The bridge to your left which crosses Mill Road is another aqueduct, it carries water to the mill's water wheel.

7. **Turn right onto Mill Road and in 250 metres you will return to the car park.**

Other Places of Interest in the Area

Cromford Mill

The world's first water-powered cotton spinning mill. Café and shops and access to the mill yard, but the mill complex is undergoing redevelopment to become a working exhibition and major visitor attraction in the future. Telephone 01629 824297 for opening dates and times.

National Tramway Museum, Crich

Extensive working collection of trams from around the world. One mile of track on which tram rides can be taken in an authentic setting. Telephone 01773 852565 for opening dates and times.

Riber Castle Wildlife Park, Riber Castle, Matlock

Collection of rare breeds and endangered species plus owls and deer. Telephone 01629 582073 for opening dates and times.

Cromford Canal Checklist

☐ A SWING-BRIDGE

☐ "ENGINES MUST NOT ENTER THIS WAREHOUSE" SIGN

☐ DUCKS

☐ IVY-COVERED TREES

☐ BARGE MOORING RINGS

☐ A QUARRY CRANE

☐ A SWAN

☐ A RAILWAY WAGON

☐ A TALL CHIMNEY

☐ SILVER BIRCH TREES

10. Dale Abbey

Dale Abbey is one of the rare rural oases in the heavily developed area between Derby and Nottingham. It has thankfully escaped the ravages of industry and housing. This is a very short walk, but it transports visitors back to the time of the crusades and provides ample interest, particularly in terms of the strange parish church and the hermit's cave.

Starting point:	The Carpenter's Arms pub, Dale Abbey (SK436 389). Dale Abbey is 8 miles west of Derby. Take the A52 towards Nottingham, and at Spondon turn onto the A6096. After approximately 3 miles, Dale Abbey is signposted to your right. Unfortunately, cars can park only on the village roads. Please show due consideration to others.
By bus:	Service from Derby to The Flourish on the A6096. Take the footpath opposite 1, The Flourish (this is the house next to The Flourish in the Ilkeston direction), which leads down and across fields to emerge, in about half a mile, beside the Gateway Christian Centre that is mentioned in point 1 of the route description.
Distance:	A short one of just 1½ miles – but a must for all!
Terrain:	Woodland and field paths across virtually flat countryside, some road walking but on minor roads.
Maps:	OS Landranger 129 and Pathfinder 833
Public Toilets:	None, but those at the Carpenter's Arms pub may be used by customers.
Refreshments:	The Carpenter's Arms pub and The Tea Rooms
Pushchairs:	Suitable, with a little effort between points 8 and 9

☺ The village takes its name from the great abbey that was built here nearly 800 years ago. In those days the area was known as 'Depedale'

1. **Walk down the road immediately opposite the Carpenter's Arms pub**

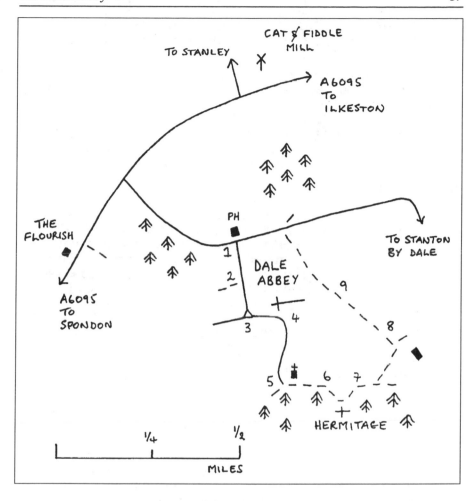

until you reach The Gateway Christian Centre (ex-Wesleyan Chapel). Here walk up the signposted footpath (actually a driveway at this point) to view the building to the rear of the Centre.

☺ These are the remains of the gate-house to Dale Abbey (you can shortly view the abbey ruins). For a period after 1538 it was used as an overnight jail when prisoners were being transported between Nottingham and Derby.

2. Return to the road and continue down to the village green.

Q: **(ON THE LEFT, MIDWAY BETWEEN THE PUB AND THE
    GREEN)** What is the date above the door of the house called
    The Bungalow?

A: 1842. This brick building looks a little out of place. It is very like
    those you would see in Northern Belgium and the neighbour-
    ing part of France.

☺ **(AT THE VILLAGE GREEN)** The lane to your right is called Tattle
    Lane and is thought to have gained its name from an area where
    people gossiped, as in the phrase "tittle tattle".

3. **Follow the road left to Abbey House.**

☺ Abbey House includes the remains of the abbey's refectory
    (dining hall). **(THE ABBEY RUINS CAN BE VIEWED BY
    CALLING AT ABBEY HOUSE).** Behind the house is the abbey's
    great eastern window arch which is 12 metres high and 5 metres
    wide. This arch and the uncovered foundations of the abbey show
    that it was a huge building. Like many other abbeys and
    monasteries in England, it ceased to be a religious centre by
    order of King Henry VIII in 1538. When the grave of one of the
    abbey's priests was opened, he was found to be lying on a bed
    of leaves still green after 600 years!

4. **Continue along the road to All Saints Church.**

☺ The left-hand part of this building is All Saints Church but the
    remainder is a farmhouse! This may seem an odd arrangement
    but in earlier times there was an even stranger one. The
    farmhouse part was then the Bluebell Inn. You could attend a
    church service and then walk through the building to have a drink.
    The church measures only 8 by 8 metres and was given its
    present form in 1480. In those days it would have had a thatched
    roof. Legend has it that the wedding of Alan-a-Dale (of Robin
    Hood fame) took place here. You can just imagine the Merry Men
    attending this church.

5. **Follow the road past the church and through the farmyard to a gate
    (ignore the path which leads off to the right just before the farm
    buildings). Pass through this and another gate to enter Hermit's
    Wood.**

Q: By the gated entrance to Hermit's Wood you should see some
    holly growing. Do all holly trees have berries?

A: No. There are male and female holly trees but only the female

The Hermit's Cave

ones have berries. Holly grows slowly and trees may be extremely old! The wood is hard and was used for making printing blocks.

🙂 Hermit's Wood was part of Sherwood Forest. The wood has a great variety of trees, shrubs and plants but most notable are the ancient limes. See if you can identify a lime tree.

6. **Shortly after entering the woods you will see some steps on your right, climb these to the Hermit's Cave.**

🙂 Between 1130 and 1140 a Derby baker by the name of Cornelius dreamt that he was told to go to Depedale to live a life of prayer and solitude. He came to this place and carved out a room with a door and windows from the sandstone. One day when Ralph Fitz-Geremund came to hunt in these woods, he felt sorry for Cornelius. He gave him the site of the hermitage and the rent from his mill at Borrowwash. With this income, the hermit was able to build a house of prayer, which was the start of All Saints Church. Later the abbey was built in memory of the hermit.

🙂 During the rest of your walk you should see a white-painted windmill on the high ground north-east of Dale Abbey. This is the Cat and Fiddle mill which unfortunately is in need of some repair. It is a rare post mill. That means that all of the building, including the milling machinery, rotates on one huge, wooden post so that the mill can follow the wind.

7. **Continue past the Hermit's Cave, descend another flight of steps and turn right to a gate giving access to pasture land. On entering the pasture, walk diagonally left to a stile which is located in the hedge just to the left of the terraced cottages.**

☺ In this pasture with its great thistles, at the edge of ancient woodland it is difficult to consider that just over a mile behind the cottages used to be the great cast iron works of Stanton. Many are the manhole covers with the name "Stanton" that were made here — the works are now much reduced. Also gone are the coal mines that lay only some two to three miles to the north. In fact, the great Derbyshire/Nottinghamshire coalfield starts from these wooded, sandstone hills and runs north all the way to and into Yorkshire.

8. **Cross the stile and make your way diagonally left across the next field to another stile located midway along the opposing hedge.**

Q: Can you identify the bushes to the right of the stile that you have just reached?

A: They are blackthorns and the small plum-shaped, blue-black berries that they bear are known as sloes. Jam and wine can be made from them.

9. **Cross the stile and, continuing on the same line, reach another one giving access to a road (Moor Lane). Turn left on this and you will shortly return to your starting point.**

Dale Abbey Checklist

☐ A LIME TREE
☐ SANDSTONE ROCK
☐ THISTLES
☐ COWS
☐ A SLOE
☐ A WINDMILL
☐ A STONE CROSS
☐ HOLLY

11. Derwent Reservoirs

The Upper Derwent valley has been transformed by the formation of the reservoirs and forestry plantations into an area of stunning beauty. The scenery is reminiscent of the Lake District or Scotland. The route visits one of the huge dams and takes you through forests to upland pastures where the scenery can be fully appreciated.

Starting point:	Fairholmes car park (SK173894) below the Derwent Dam. The dam is 12 miles west of Sheffield and is clearly signposted from the A57.
By bus:	Limited daily service from Sheffield, summer Sundays from Buxton and summer Saturdays and Sundays from Bakewell.
Distance:	Entire route 4 miles
Terrain:	Mostly footpaths and forest/farm tracks. A climb from Derwent Dam to Lockerbrook Farm but nothing excessive.
Maps:	OS Outdoor Leisure Sheet 1
Public Toilets:	Fairholmes car park. There are baby changing facilities.
Refreshments:	Light refreshments at the kiosk next to the National Park Visitor Centre, Fairholmes car park.
Pushchairs:	Unsuitable

(Fairholmes Visitor Centre has displays covering the history, flora and fauna of the Upper Derwent Valley. Particular coverage of the dam's construction, water supply system and association with the Dambusters. There is also a cycle hire shop in the complex.)

1.   At the entrance to the lower Fairholmes car park, take the footpath signposted Derwent Dam. This path descends and shortly meets a road. Turn right on to this and follow it to the Derwent River Bridge.

☺ **(AT THE BRIDGE)** This is the Derwent river. In the days of the Saxons (409 – 1066AD) it was known as "dwr gwent", which means "white water". As the name suggests, the river, before the dams were built, could be a raging torrent after a storm or heavy rain. Over the years it has cut this valley through extremely hard rock known as gritstone.

2.   **Without crossing the bridge turn left and follow the ascending foot-path (ignore the path which enters from the left) to the main valley road. Here turn right to the dam.**

☺ This is the Derwent Dam and one of three built in this valley. The others are called Howden and Ladybower. The Derwent and Howden dams were completed in 1916, and the Ladybower in the 1940s. Their reservoirs supply water to the cities of Sheffield, Derby, Nottingham and Leicester. The Derwent Dam is 35 metres high and 54 metres thick at its base. The half million tonnes of gritstone used to build this dam were transported here by a railway which has since been removed. Each block of stone weighs 6 tonnes.

☺ If you look inside the entrance to the dam you will see memorials to the Dambusters. During the Second World War Royal Air Force air crew and their planes destroyed similar dams in Germany. They used a special

The Derwent Dam

type of bomb that bounced along the reservoir's surface and then exploded against the dam. The Howden and Derwent dams were used to train the air crew.

3. From the dam continue along the roadside path to Tip's monument.

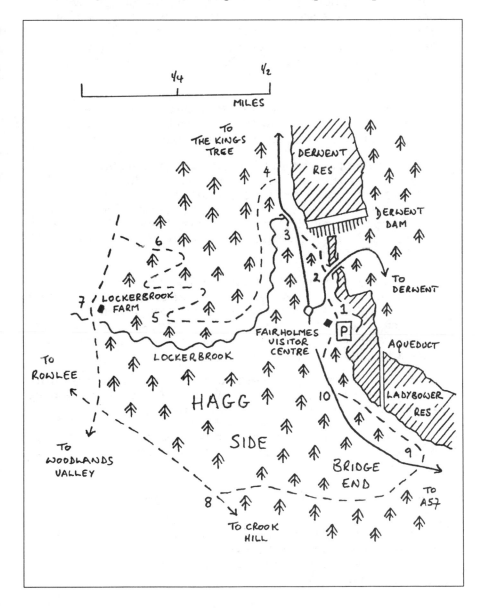

Q: Near the Derwent dam there is a memorial to Tip. Who was this and what did Tip do?

A: Tip was a sheep dog who, in the winter of 1953/54, kept watch for 15 weeks beside her 86-year-old master, Joe Tagg, who had died in the deep snow on Howden Moors. Howden Moors are the wilderness above the opposite bank of this reservoir. Tip was very ill when she was found, but was nursed back to health and received a bronze medal for her devotion. Unfortunately, she died in 1955 and is buried on the moors where she kept her vigil.

4. **Continue along the roadside path to a cattle grid. Here cross the road and follow the forest track with a concessionary footpath sign as it slowly winds up through the trees (ignore the side paths).**

☺ Most of the forest has been planted since the construction of the Derwent and Howden dams. Fortunately, the planting has included both coniferous (cone-bearing) and broad-leaved trees. In warm weather there is a beautiful forest aroma. The soil is very acidic and this is highlighted by the type of plants that grow here — especially ferns and foxgloves, with their tall columns of pink hood-shaped flowers.

☺ How many types of broad-leaved trees can you spot? During your journey through the forests you should see oak, beech, sycamore and birch. You should also see many forest-loving birds — in particular, the crossbill. As the name suggests this bird has a crossed beak which it uses to pull its principal food, pine seeds, from within the pine cones.

5. **Shortly after a sharp right-hand bend you will see a signpost on your right. Here turn sharp left and follow the forest path all the way up to a stile on the edge of the forest.**

☺ On the path notice that the ground is covered with a thick layer of pine needles and that some of the tree roots are above the surface of the soil.

Q: Why are there no plants in this part of the forest?

A: Because the trees are planted so close together that they shut out the daylight to the forest floor. Notice that the trees' lower needles have either turned brown or been lost due to the lack of light. As you reach more open planting, the forest floor again becomes green.

6. **Cross the stile and continue straight up towards the next one, which gives access to an unsurfaced farm track (end of the concessionary path). Turn left on to this and follow it to Lockerbrook Farm.**

☺ Can you see the Ladybower reservoir far below you? On the ridge above the opposite bank you should see groups of odd-shaped rocks. These have descriptive names such as The Salt Cellar, Cakes of Bread etc. They have been shaped by the action of wind and rain. The ridge is the boundary between Derbyshire and Yorkshire.

7. **Pass the farm, now keeping the edge of a forest on your left to reach a junction above the Woodlands Valley. Here turn left, pass over a stile and follow the track signposted Crook Hill.**

☺ **(ON THE TRACK)** The track that you are following is the old packhorse route between Glossop and Sheffield. In the valley below you is the route's replacement — the Snake Pass built in 1821. This is often closed during the winter by snow drifts.

8. **At the next stile and gate turn left following the sign 'Bridgend Car Park/Derwent Valley'. This path leads down through the forest to meet the valley road. Cross this road and turn left onto the concessionary path which follows the shore line of the reservoir.**

☺ When the Ladybower Reservoir was built, the village of Derwent was flooded. At very low water levels some of the village ruins may be seen. They are near the far bank, where the Mill Brook enters the reservoir. The packhorse route that you have just descended used to cross the Derwent River by a 17th-century bridge. This has been rebuilt at the head of the valley at a place known as Slippery Stones. The packhorse route went up the opposite bank and over the ridge to Sheffield.

☺ On the water and along the shore line see how many different types of wildfowl birds you can spot? Depending on the season and the height of the water you should see Canada geese with their long black necks and white throats, mallard ducks and goosanders, the females have grey bodies and a rust-coloured head.

9. **Follow the path over a number of small, wooden bridges and past the end of an aqueduct to rejoin the road.**

☺ **(AT THE AQUEDUCT)** This bridge carries two huge water pipes across the reservoir and is called an aqueduct. The water comes from the Howden and Derwent dams and is on its way to Sheffield, Derby, Nottingham and Leicester.

10. **On reaching the road turn right and follow it back to the Fairholmes car park.**

☺ While the adults are resting you may fancy feeding the birds that live around the picnic area. Remember birds should not eat excessive amounts of salt so AVOID SALTED PEANUTS and CRISPS. They can eat bread, cheese, cake, biscuits, meat scraps and fruit. However, if all your picnic has been eaten you may wish to buy a small bag of seed from the tea kiosk. Ducks also enjoy a nibble but they prefer brown bread! *Remember to break the unsalted peanuts into small pieces as the birds may feed them to their small chicks and cause them to choke!*

Derwent Reservoir Checklist

☐ AN OAK TREE

☐ A RHODODENDRON

☐ A SQUIRREL

☐ A FINCH

☐ A CATTLE GRID

☐ A DUCK

☐ A SPRING (WATER)

☐ A SHEEP

☐ A CANADA GOOSE

☐ AN AQUEDUCT

12. Earl Sterndale

The walk out from Earl Sterndale takes you through a typical upland limestone landscape which, on approaching the height known as High Edge, is very reminiscent of the Yorkshire Dales around Ingleborough. The return is initially through gritstone country with fine views of the fledgling River Dove right up to the long ridge of Axe Edge. Finally, the Dove valley opens up with a magnificent panorama of jagged peaks which were once coral reefs.

Starting point: The village green, Earl Sterndale (SK091 670). The village is 5 miles south-east of Buxton. Take the A515 towards Ashbourne and at Brierlow Bar turn on to the B5053. After approximately 1½ miles, Earl Sterndale is signposted to your left. Unfortunately, cars can be parked only on the village roads. Please show due consideration for others.

By bus: Service from Buxton (no winter Sunday service).

Distance: Entire route 5 miles. Shorter route 2½ miles.

Terrain: Mostly upland paths and tracks across grazing land with some walking on minor roads.

Maps: OS Outdoor Leisure Sheet 24

Public Toilets: None, but those at the Quiet Woman pub may be used by customers.

Refreshments: The Quiet Woman pub, Earl Sterndale

Pushchairs: Unsuitable

☺ This is the village of Earl Sterndale. "Sterndale" simply means "stony ground" and is a good description of the area. Earl suggests that at one time it belonged to the Earl of Derby. During World War II the church was, unfortunately, bombed and virtually destroyed. The air crew were either having to shed their deadly cargo or had misjudged the bombing of the now abandoned ammunition stores located in the hills south of Buxton.

1. **With your back to the Quiet Woman pub, follow the road immediately to your left down to a crossroads.**

Q: What is growing on the drystone walls as you approach the crossroads?

A: Moss. In places it is very thick and nearly covers the walls.

2. **Continue straight ahead at the crossroads and follow the road past two houses until you reach a track to your left.**

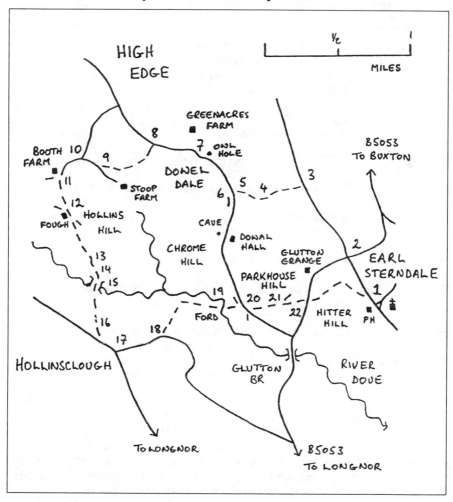

☺ After passing the house called Hatch A Way you should notice that the drystone walls have various species of yellow and silver-coloured lichen growing upon them. Lichen will not grow in polluted air.

3. **Turn left onto the track and follow it to a stile on your right. Cross the stile and immediately turn left. Now follow the right-hand side of a wall to a stile in the top corner of the pasture.**

☺ The rock in this area is limestone. It was formed 330 million years ago when this area was under the sea.

Q: Of what is limestone formed?

A: The remains of millions of sea creatures. Where rock has recently been broken away you may see some of their fossilised remains.

4. **Cross the stile and pasture, keeping parallel with the hillside wall to your right, to reach another stile above Dowel Dale.**

☺ This is Dowel Dale. At some time in the past its river would have been seen above ground but it has found weaknesses in the limestone, allowing it to follow an underground route.

☺ Sheep often graze on these steep slopes. They sometimes appear to play a game of Dare when they walk out to the very edge of the rock face.

Woolly jumpers in Dowel Dale

5. Cross the stile and descend the slope to reach a roadside stile.

Q: What type of tree do you pass whilst descending to the road?

A: An ash tree. Ash is extremely strong and was used to make carts and the frames of early cars.

Escape route: Turn left and follow the road downhill past Dowal Hall and Chrome and Parkhouse hills to where a track enters right from the Stannery. Here rejoin the main route at point 20.

☺ On reaching Dowal Hall look to your right to discover the emergence of the river that has been flowing beneath Dowel Dale. Near here is a cave which is known to have been occupied by Stone Age man, who had to hunt for food. His hunting ground would have been the Dove Valley which you are entering.

6. Turn right onto the road and follow it uphill until just short of a cattle grid.

☺ **(INDICATE THE LARGE, FENCED OFF HOLE ON THE RIGHT, JUST BEFORE THE CATTLE GRID)** This is Owl Hole and has been fenced off for your safety. It is one of several points hereabouts where water leaves ground level to form the river running below Dowel Dale. It is called a sink hole.

7. Pass the cattle grid and continue along the road via another grid to reach a track on your left.

☺ Notice some further sink holes in the fields on either side of the road. In front of you is the long ridge of High Edge which rises to 1430 feet (436 metres). Beneath its northern face lies an abandoned World War II ammunition store.

8. Turn left on to the track leading to Stoop Farm and follow it past another cattle grid. Here take the path signed Booth Farm which departs right from the farm track. Keeping Stoop Farm and its surrounding trees to your right, descend to a stile giving access to another farm track.

9. Cross this and follow the track away from Stoop Farm to meet a road junction at yet another cattle grid.

☺ On the skyline ahead of you there is the long ridge of Axe Edge, 1800 feet (549 metres), which is one of the highest points in Derbyshire. Axe Edge and the surrounding moors are the source of a number of rivers. Here start the Dove, Manifold and Wye rivers whose waters will reach the North Sea; and the Dane and Goyt heading for the Irish Sea at Liverpool.

10. **Turn left onto the road and follow it to a junction just short of Booth Farm.**

☺ As you walk along this road observe how the types of stone used in the building of the roadside walls change. At first the wall is made of limestone, but as you approach Booth Farm this is replaced with gritstone. The change in building materials reflects the change in the rocks over which you are walking. You have now entered gritstone country. Gritstone was formed some 230 million years ago when this area was the delta of a great river flowing from a land of which Scotland formed part. The name "Booth" suggests that originally there was a shelter here that protected domestic animals from attack by either wild animals or thieves.

11. **At the road junction, take the left-hand fork via a cattle grid. The track is signed "Fough", pronounced "Foo". Follow it along the right-hand side of Hollins Hill until you approach a house.**

Q: What is the dark green, prickly plant that grows on these hillsides? In summer it has bright yellow flowers.

A: It is gorse or furze.

12. **Pass to the left of the house and at the next junction follow the right-hand, descending grass track.**

13. **At the next junction keep right and continue your descent via a gate/stile to a sandy path on your right.**

☺ You are now approaching the River Dove. Notice the lush vegetation that follows the river. Here can be found silver birch, rowan, beech, wild rose, foxglove with their pink hood-shaped flowers, bilberry and many other plants and trees.

14. **Turn right onto the path and follow it down to a gate which gives access to a bridge.**

☺ This is an old packhorse bridge and in crossing it and the River Dove, you have entered Staffordshire. This is a good place to cool your toes. Can you see the water gauge under the bridge?

15. **Cross the bridge and follow the path diagonally left up the grass slope. This path becomes enclosed shortly before reaching a roadside gate.**

☺ The view downstream is wonderful, particularly of Chrome Hill (the one to your left shaped like a dragon's back) and its neighbour Parkhouse Hill. These limestone hills were once coral reefs.

16. **Turn left onto the road into the village of Hollinsclough.**

☺ This is the village of Hollinsclough. Silk was once woven in the cottages here as part of the industry focused on the Macclesfield (Cheshire) mills.

Q: What is the date on the Methodist chapel (Bethel) located at the road junction?

A: 1804. The initials refer to John Lomas, the local preacher at the time.

17. **At the road junction turn left and follow the road past the old school to a track on your left.**

☺ **(INDICATE THE OLD SCHOOL)** This building was the original village school. You may notice that it is also dated 1804.

18. **Turn left onto the track and follow this across the meadows to a junction just short of the River Dove. Keep right, following the river, until you reach a ford and footbridge.**

☺ This old ford takes you back into Derbyshire. Prior to the building of the footbridge you would have had to get your feet wet.

19. **Cross the bridge and follow the track to reach a road. Ignore the track that joins you from the right, which serves the Stannery.**

20. **Turn right onto the road** *(the escape route rejoins the main route here)* **and follow this to a yellow-painted stile on your right. Here head diagonally left across the grass to a yellow-painted boulder.**

21. **Continue forward and across a series of yellow-painted stiles to a road (B5053).**

☺ The farmhouse to your left is called Glutton Grange and it bears the date 1675. It is said that cattle were hidden here from soldiers in 1745, but they were found. The soldiers had a huge feast hence the name "Glutton".

22. **Cross the road and the opposing stile and climb diagonally left up the side of Hitter Hill. Again crossing yellow-marked stiles and following the yellow marks. After the summit the path crosses a**

couple of grazing fields to a field gate and stile giving access to the road on which you first set out.

☺ Hitter Hill, the side of which you have just crossed, and the two hills immediately to the east (Aldery Cliff and High Wheeldon) are also old coral reefs. High Wheeldon, the pyramid shaped hill to the east of Earl Sterndale, was given to the nation as a memorial to the men of Staffordshire and Derbyshire who died in World War II.

Other Places Of Interest In The Area

Poole's Cavern and Buxton Country Park

A 40 hectare park with panoramic views and a show cave known as Poole's Cavern. There is a visitor centre and shop. Telephone 01298 26978 for opening dates and times.

Earl Sterndale Checklist

☐ A YELLOW-PAINTED STILE

☐ A VICTORIAN LETTERBOX

☐ A ROWAN TREE

☐ A CATTLE GRID

☐ A ROADSIDE STREAM

☐ GORSE

☐ A SINK HOLE

☐ A SHEEP

☐ A FORD

☐ FERNS

13. Elvaston Castle Country Park

On the River Derwent meadows, south-east of Derby, lies Elvaston Castle. It is surrounded by an estate which has managed to maintain its tranquillity despite the intense urban and industrial development of the Derby/Nottingham corridor. Derbyshire County Council bought the property in 1960 and it now forms a 90 hectare country park. The castle itself is not open to the public but there is a lake and forest, both of which abound with bird life, formal gardens, parkland for picnics (at point 9 there is a "picnic spot" for waterfowl !) and ball games.

Starting point: Elvaston Castle Country Park car park (SK412 332). Elvaston Castle is 5 miles south-east of Derby and is clearly signposted from the A6. The park and car park are open during daylight hours throughout the year. There is a parking charge.

By bus: Services from Derby, Loughborough and Leicester to the start of the castle's main drive on the A6 (on buses this is the Golden Gates stop). Walk up the drive to the Golden Gates and start from point 10 of the route description.

Distance: Entire route 1¾ miles

Terrain: Virtually flat. Mostly paths through parkland, gardens and woodland. Some quiet, estate road walking.

Maps: OS Landranger 129 and Pathfinder 833

Public Toilets: In the car park and beside the Information Centre at Elvaston Castle.

Refreshments: Mrs Kemp's Tea Rooms at the Castle

Pushchairs: Totally suitable

1. Walk through the car park to the park's main pedestrian entrance. Without leaving the car park, turn right and follow its perimeter with woodland to your left. When the woodland gives way to open parkland, leave the car park and follow the path along the parkland/woodland boundary to a field gate at the start of a woodland track.

Elvaston Castle

☺ On both sides of the path you will find wooden structures for physical exercise. See how fit you are by trying them out.

2. **Pass round the field gate and immediately turn left through a fence gap into the woods. Follow the woodland path to a seat just short of the lakeside.**

☺ The woods are home to a wide variety of birds. According to the season, you should spot nuthatches – the sparrow-sized woodpecker, redpole – the sparrow with a red forehead and pink breast, tits and woodpeckers. Nesting boxes have been attached to the trees, the larger ones are for tawny owls. In the woods you may also see grey squirrels.

Q: What is the home of a squirrel called?

A: A drey. They build these in the forks of tree branches by using woodland floor debris.

3. **Now turn right, keeping the lake to your left, and continue through the woods until reaching a gate. Pass through this and turn left onto a track to immediately reach a concrete bridge.**

☺ The lake has been formed by the damming of a small stream which is part of the River Derwent. You may be lucky and see some waterfowl, but most of them gather beside the castle as this is where the visitors feed them. You will come to their "picnic site" later in the walk.

4. **Cross the bridge and follow the track to a T-junction in front of the castle's stables.**
   (In the courtyard to your left there is an information centre and toilets.)

5. **Here turn right onto an estate road and pass between the ornamental gateposts.**

☺ **(INDICATE THE BUILDING ON THE RIGHT JUST BEFORE THE GATEPOSTS)** The odd-shaped building on the right is called Springthorpe Cottage. It was built by the owner of the castle, the Earl of Harrington, hence the large letter "H" above the door. He enjoyed constructing such fantasy buildings and you will come across another, The Mill, later on this walk.

   (Elvaston Castle Museum – for details see "Other Places of Interest in the Area".)

6. **Follow the estate road, at first via duckboards, to where a track enters from the right. Here bear left with the road to pass a cricket pitch.**

Q: How long is a cricket pitch?

A: 22 yards (20 metres).

☺ The fields either side of the road are home to a number of horses and ponies. Remember if you feed them to place the food on the palm of your hand, keeping it flat. They do not wish to eat your fingers as well as the food.

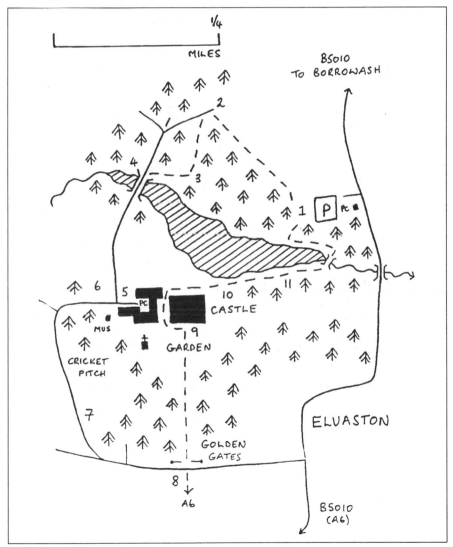

7. Continue along the estate road (ignore the track that enters from the right), past the church road (left), until you reach the so-called Golden Gates.

☺ These gates are called the Golden Gates although they are mostly painted blue! They were brought here from the Palace of Versailles, France, in 1819 by the 3rd Earl of Harrington.

8. Turn left through the Golden Gates and follow the tree-lined path to a tree arch. Pass under this and through the formal gardens to the castle.

Q: **(AT THE ARCH)** Can you identify the type of tree that has been used to form this arch?

A: They are yews, which were originally trained and cut to form a huge crown. Derbyshire County Council are trying to restore the gardens to their former glory.

☺ The garden in front of the castle is called a parterre. It is formed from box trees that have been cut into very small hedges. The hedges produce a geometric pattern.

☺ The castle is, in fact, a large house with decorative battlements and turrets. It was given its present shape in 1817. The brickwork that can be seen on this side of the house dates from 1633.

9. Turn left and walk round the castle, through the courtyard and across the lawns to the lake.

☺ This is the "picnic spot" for the lake's waterfowl. Some of them have become extremely tame and will come to you looking for food. You should see Canada geese with their black necks and white throats, and pintail, shoveler and tufted ducks.

10. Turn right along the lakeside to follow a path through the trees and past artificial rock formations to reach a small watermill.

☺ These rocks were brought here and built into various shapes to beautify the gardens. Can you find the group of rocks with the "Polo Mint" hole?

☺ **(AT THE MILL)** This is another one of the odd-shaped buildings to be found around the estate. It still has its small waterwheel, but unfortunately it no longer works.

11. Continue along the lakeside and cross its outflow to a path junction. Here turn right into the car park.

Other Places of Interest in the Area

Derby Industrial Museum

Located in the Full Street Silk Mill, the museum features the two main industries of the city – aero-engine design and construction (Rolls Royce) and railway works. Telephone 01332 255308 for opening dates and times.

Elvaston Castle Estate Museum

A working museum which demonstrates the life, work and skills of a country estate. Staff are in period costume. Telephone 01332 573799 for opening dates and times.

Elvaston Castle Checklist

☐ A CYCLIST

☐ A CLOCK TOWER

☐ A DUCK

☐ STABLES

☐ A CRICKET PLAYER

☐ A SQUIRREL

☐ A GOOSE

☐ A BIRD NESTING BOX

☐ A YEW TREE

☐ DUCKBOARDS

14. Goyt Valley

It is hard to believe that this jewel of a valley is only twenty miles from central Manchester. Since the completion of the second reservoir, the valley above Fernlee Dam is uninhabited and it is extremely difficult to imagine that a village, farms, paint and gunpowder factories all once flourished here. This walk takes you around Errwood Reservoir and along the infant River Goyt through woodland and moors. The experience of the moors with just the sound of the wind and birds and the view of sail boats is wonderful.

Starting point: The Street car park, Errwood Reservoir (SK013 756). The reservoir is 3 miles north-west of Buxton. Follow the Goyt Valley signs at Long Hill, on the A5004, down and across Errwood Dam to the car park.

Distance: Entire route 4½ miles

Terrain: Woodland and moorland tracks/paths with some road walking. Can be boggy between points 10 and 11.

Maps: OS Outdoor Leisure Sheet 24

Public Toilets: At Bunsal Cob car park just east of the Errwood Dam and Goyt's Clough Quarry car park near Goyt's Bridge.

Refreshments: None

Pushchairs: Suitable between points 1 and 8 (keeping to the road) as a linear route. Ideal when the road south of the Street car park is closed to traffic (Sundays and Bank Holidays from May to September). About 3 miles in total.

1. **From the car park entrance turn right and follow the road south (keeping Errwood Reservoir on your left) to Errwood car park.**

2. **At the rear of the car park take the path that leads up to the top left-hand corner of the grassland. Here, ignoring the path rising from your left, continue uphill to meet a track.**

☺ This is Errwood Reservoir which was completed in 1968. With Fernlee Reservoir further down the valley, up to 9 billion litres of water can be stored for supply to Stockport and the surrounding

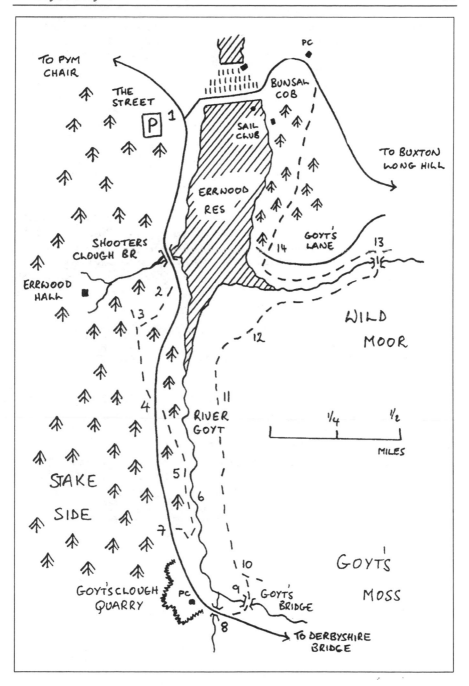

area. In constructing the reservoir the village of Goyt's Bridge had to be abandoned. The submerged ruins of the village are located almost in front of the Errwood car park and at low water levels they re-emerge. Until 1928 the River Goyt formed the county boundary and the west bank, that you are now on, belonged to Cheshire.

3. **Turn left onto the track and follow it until you reach a road.**

☺ In this area you should keep a sharp watch for pheasants. They love wandering amongst the ground cover just over the drystone wall to your left and they sometimes venture out into the open area, or may even perch on the wall.

☺ Notice that the walls here are constructed from very dark stone. This is gritstone and it is the upper layer of rock throughout this area. It was formed some 230 million years ago when this whole area was the delta of a great river flowing from a land of which Scotland formed a part. When the rock is first cut it has a golden brown colour but this soon weathers to the colour you see in the walls.

4. **Cross the road and take the forest track opposite which runs above to the west bank of the River Goyt.**
    (If you prefer to stay on the road turn right and continue the walk at point 7.)

☺ The forest that you are passing through has many oak and beech trees. Can you identify them?

Q: What are the fruits of these two types of trees called?

A: The fruit of the oak is an acorn and that of the beech is a mast. Whilst oaks fruit annually, beech trees produce fruit only once in every four to five years. Both trees are used to make furniture but for many years oak provided the frame for houses and the navy constructed their ships from it. Some 40 000 tonnes of oak were needed to build a 75 gun war ship.

☺ In the woods here you should find many types of fungi, particularly where fallen timber has rotted. See if you can identify the various types. **DO NOT PICK OR TOUCH ANY FUNGI AS SOME ARE POISONOUS.**

5. **The forest track eventually deteriorates to a path. Here continue forward and across a series of side streams to reach the Goyt at river level.**

☺ This is the River Goyt which rises at the base of a long-ridged hill known as Axe Edge, some 1½ miles south of here. Its waters reach the Irish Sea at Liverpool. Over the years the river has cut its way down through the peat and gritstone and has created a wonderful place to paddle!.

6. **Continue along the riverbank and cross another side stream (this requires some nimble footwork) to reach some steps on your right. Climb these and bear left through some bracken to a road.**

7. **Turn left onto the road and follow it past Goyt's Clough Quarry car park.**

☺ This is Goyt's Clough Quarry, which at one time supplied most of the paving slabs for London. The quarry was worked by the Pickford family from the 17th century. They used packhorse trains, each consisting of 50 horses, to transport the slabs. The horses used to return without a cargo, which was uneconomic. Pickfords advertised to carry cargo on any part of the journey back from London and so the worldwide road haulage firm of Pickfords was founded.

Goyt's Bridge

8. **Follow the road over a stream (Deep Clough) and turn left down a path to a packhorse bridge.**

☺ This packhorse bridge is at least 300 years old. It was moved here from the village of Goyt's Bridge when Errwood Reservoir was constructed. The bridge originally lay on a route used by packhorse trains transporting salt across the Pennine Hills from Cheshire.

9. **Cross the bridge and follow the path diagonally left, up the river bank to a path T-junction.**

☺ The ground here is covered with bracken, a non-flowering, fern-like plant that turns brown in the autumn. Unless cut back the bracken will gradually take over vast areas of these moors.

10. **Here turn left and follow the path way mark "4". This again runs through bracken and then a mixture of bracken and heather. The whole area is covered in a thick layer of peat which in places can be boggy.**

☺ The black or dark brown soil here is peat. It is composed of layer upon layer of moss. 7500 years ago the climate in this area changed and allowed the moss to grow. As one plant died, another grew on top of it. Thus a mass of dead but not decomposed moss was produced. Unfortunately, since the Industrial Revolution the atmosphere is slowly destroying the peat.

11. **After crossing the remnants of three walls the path continues along the left- hand side of a virtually unbroken wall (way marks with the number '4' or a yellow arrow on them appear at frequent intervals along this route). When another wall blocks your progress turn diagonally right through a gap and resume your direction, but now with a wall on your left.**

☺ You are now on the grass moorlands where you may see butterflies such as the painted lady (its wings are brick red with black and white patches on the points of the forewings). They come from North Africa and lay their eggs in the thistle heads.

12. **Cross a stream and climb up to a track. Here turn left and follow the track down to a bridge across Wildmoorstone Brook.**

13. **At the far side of the bridge turn left and follow the track to a path/track crossroads.**

☺ **(AT THE CROSSROADS)** The track coming downhill from your right and continuing into the reservoir is known as Goyt's Lane. This was the old road from Buxton to Goyt's Bridge village.

14. **Cross Goyt's Lane following the path signposted Bunsal Cob. This path works its way across a series of grassed areas which are separated by conifer plantations until it reaches a road.**

☺ The road that you have now reached has been built on the trackbed of a former railway. The railway was known as the Cromford and High Peak Railway and ran from Cromford in the Derwent valley to Whaley Bridge. This section was known as Bunsal Incline and had a gradient of 1 in 7. It was opened in 1831 and closed 61 years later when an easier route was constructed east of Long Hill.

15. **Turn left onto the road and follow it down and across Errwood Dam to your starting point.**

☺ At the far end of the dam there is a bronze plaque which gives the dam's statistics.

☺ The road ascending the hill away from your car park is known as The Street. It is believed to be the northern extension of the Roman Road from Derby to Buxton.

Goyt Valley Checklist

☐ A BUTTERFLY

☐ A TV/RADIO TRANSMITTER

☐ A RAILWAY MONUMENT

☐ BEECH MAST

☐ A SAILBOAT

☐ PICNIC TABLES

☐ PHEASANTS

☐ FUNGI

15. Longshaw Estate and Hathersage Moor

The high moorland that forms the Derbyshire/Yorkshire border south-west of Sheffield was for many years the private domain of the Duke of Rutland and his guests. It was specifically kept for the rearing and shooting of grouse. The route, based on the old shooting lodge, takes you across the stunningly beautiful Hathersage Moor which is reminiscent of the Scottish Highlands.

Starting point: Woodcroft car park, Longshaw Lodge (SK226 802). The Lodge is 7½ miles south-west of Sheffield and is clearly signposted from the A625 at the Fox House Inn. There is no public access to the lodge itself but the estate is permanently open.

By bus: Services form Sheffield, Bakewell and Hathersage and Grindleford rail stations to the Fox House Inn. Pedestrian gate opposite the inn leads to the Lodge Drive. Turn left on this and start the walk from the "Lodge Drive" part of point 1.

Distance: Entire route 4¼ miles. Shorter route 1¾ miles.

Terrain: Mostly moorland paths and tracks. A little climbing through and across rocks, but nothing excessive. Can be boggy between point 10 and Carl Wark.

Maps: Outdoor Leisure Sheets 1 and 24

Public Toilets: Beside the Visitor Centre, Longshaw Lodge

Refreshments: Teas and light lunches at the Visitor Centre, Longshaw Lodge. Fox House Inn.

Pushchairs: Only suitable between points 1 to 4 and 14 to 1 but a complete circular route of 1½ miles can be achieved by following the pavement along the B6521 from point 4 to 14.

1. **From the car park, follow the downhill path which, on reaching the tree line, crosses a bridge and joins another path. Here turn right and then cross the lodge drive to another path. Now swing left with that path and pass in front of the lodge garden.**

😊 The lodge was built in 1830 by the Duke of Rutland for grouse shooting parties and was used for that purpose until 1927 when it became the property of the National Trust. Apart from the lodge and its grounds the duke owned some 4,500 hectares in this area which were devoted to grouse shooting.

😊 The path in front of the lodge garden runs in a type of ditch which is known as a Ha-Ha. It provides a barrier to animals, but cannot

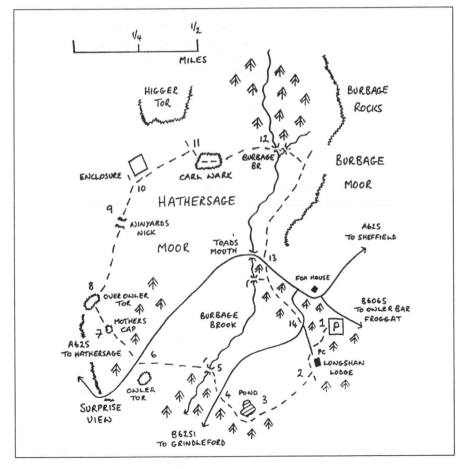

be seen from the lodge. The name comes from the surprise that it gives when discovered

2. **At the end of the Ha-Ha pass through the gate and turn right. Now follow the gentle descent along the shrub-lined path to a pond.**

Q: Do you know what the shrubs either side of this path are called?

A: They are rhododendrons and they are related to the heather that you will shortly see covering the moors. The purple-flowered rhododendron is not native to England. They were originally brought from Spain and Portugal.

3. **Follow the path around the pond and down to a gate on the B6521 (Fox House to Grindleford road).**

☺ The woods here are the north-west part of Sherwood Forest and they abound with bird life. Look out for nuthatches which look like small woodpeckers — blue-grey colouring above and buff below, finches and treecreepers — brown above and silvery white below with a fine down-curved bill.

4. **Pass through the gate and with care cross the road to another gate. Pass through this and descend to the bridge across the Burbage Brook.**

Q: Can you recognise the trees lining the bank of this brook?

A: They are alders and the fruits are borne within small egg-shaped cones. The black and empty cones are from previous years. They remain until detached by the effect of wind and rain. The new fruit arrives after the growth of catkins.

Escape route: Turn right after crossing the bridge and follow the brook to reach another footbridge. Cross this and follow the path, steps at first, up through the woods to point 14, ignoring all paths to the left.

5. **Cross the bridge and bear right to follow the pronounced sunken path up to a kissing gate on the A625 (Sheffield to Castleton road).**

☺ This sunken path used to be part of the old bridleway between Chesterfield/Dronfield and Hope. It is known as Hollow Gate.

6. **Pass through the gate and cross the road to a stile (you are now in Yorkshire). Once over the stile make your way up through the gritstone rocks to the rock tor known as either Mother's Cap or The Cocked Hat.**

☺ As you climb up and across the rocks you will pass an unfinished

Tortoise Rock, Hathersage Moor

millstone and then reach the rim of an abandoned quarry. The quarry contains millstones in various stages of production. Up to 200 years ago these hills and moors would have echoed with the sound of men chiselling these stones from the rocks. The stones were used to grind corn and put edges on the cutlery and blades made in Sheffield.

☺ Just after the quarry you should see another unfinished millstone where the surrounding rocks have been worn into interesting shapes. Can you find one looking like a smiling tortoise?

☺ **(AT THE TOR)** This huge rock is known as Mother's Cap or Cocked Hat Tor. Does it look like either of these objects to you? It and others in this area have been formed by the action of wind, rain and ice (weathering) over the last 230 million years.

7. **Walk around the tor and follow the well defined path to Over Owler Tor.**

☺ The view from Over Owler Tor is extensive. Below you is the village of Hathersage, visited by the author Charlotte Brontë. She based her novel *Jane Eyre* on this area. The village is also claimed to be the last resting place of Little John of Robin Hood fame. Behind Hathersage can be seen the Hope Valley which is surrounded by a succession of hills of which Kinder Scout, to the north-west, is the greatest height at 2077 feet (633 metres).

8. **Now follow the ridge path north to Winyards Nick (you should easily recognise this point from the deep cutting in the ridge which accommodates a crossing bridle road).**

☺ As you walk along the ridge look out for red grouse. Try not to walk through the heather itself as this is where the grouse make their nests. The heather is regularly burnt by the gamekeepers to encourage new shoots to grow. These provide food for the grouse.

9. **Continue along the ridge path to a walled enclosure.**

☺ In front of you is the highest tor in this area. It is called Higger Tor and it rises to 1260 feet (384 metres). Notice the great block of stone that leans out from the rock face.

10. **Turn right and follow the drystone wall until it turns away to the left. Here make your way to the path running along the dip between Higger Tor and the adjacent tor known as Carl Wark. On reaching the path, turn right and climb up to the summit of Carl Wark.**

☺ This 1 hectare flat-topped tor is known as Carl Wark. It was fortified by Iron Age man, and as you climb up to its summit you pass part of those fortifications – a stone wall 30 metres long and nearly 3 metres high.

11. **At the eastern end of the plateau look for, and carefully follow, a path that leads down to a packhorse bridge. The bridge is at the right of the conifer plantation.**

☺ **(AT THE BRIDGE)** This is the old Sheffield to Hathersage bridle road crossing of the Burbage Brook. Travelling these roads must have been very lonely and dangerous, particularly in winter when everything was covered by snow. Travellers had to find their way by recognising physical features such as Carl Walk and Winyards Nick.

12. **Cross the bridge and another small water course then head up the slope to reach the clearly defined crossing track known as the Duke's Drive. It runs below and parallel to the cliffs. Here turn right and follow the drive to the A625 (Sheffield to Castleton road).**

☺ This track is one of a number built by the Duke of Rutland which provided access to his grouse moors for their management and shooting parties. It is known as a Duke's Drive.

☺ The gritstone cliffs (edges) above the Duke's Drive, are often used by rock-climbers. Can you see any? The edges have been quarried in places and the rock face is constantly being broken away by winter ice.

13. **Cross the road to a gate (you have re-entered Derbyshire), pass through this and follow the path that tends left. After a short while this is joined by a path from the right and the combined path then continues through the woods to a gate giving access to the B6521 (Fox House to Grindleford road).**

14. **Cross this road to Longshaw Lodge drive *(the escape and pushchair routes rejoin here.)* and follow it back to the visitor centre, at the rear of which is your starting point.**

☺ **(POINT OUT THE WAYMARK STONE AS YOU ENTER THE DRIVE. THIS IS BEHIND THE ESTATE MAP ON YOUR THE RIGHT)** This waymark stone was placed here in 1709 when the spot was the crossing of the bridle roads to Sheffield, Tideswell, Chesterfield, Hathersage and Chapel en le Frith. Notice the incorrect spelling of the destinations. They have been spelled according to how they sounded to the person who carved the stone.

Longshaw Estate and Hathersage Moor Checklist

☐ AN ALDER

☐ SHEEP

☐ RHODODENDRONS

☐ GROUSE

☐ A STONE WAYMARK

☐ A CLIMBER

☐ HEATHER

☐ A CONIFER PLANTATION

☐ TV and RADIO TRANSMITTER

16. Melbourne and Breedon On The Hill

South of Derby and the Trent river, Derbyshire is mainly gentle, rolling farmland dotted with ancient settlements. One of the prettiest of these is Melbourne with its Norman church and Hall picturesquely set beside a lake known as the Pool. The walk loops into Leicestershire and visits Breedon on the Hill, with its church perched on what appears to be a cliff top. The return is via the Pool itself with its abundant wildfowl.

Starting point: The Church of St Michael, Melbourne (SK389 250). Melbourne is 8 miles south of Derby and is clearly signposted from the A514. The church is in the south-east part of the village, just off the road to Wilson. There is car parking against Melbourne Hall's perimeter wall, opposite the church.

By bus: Services from Derby to the Market Place, Melbourne, then a short walk down Church Street brings you to the walk's starting point.

Distance: Entire route 4¾ miles. Shorter route 1¼ miles.

Terrain: Mostly footpaths across rolling arable and grazing land. Short but not excessive climb to Breedon Church.

Maps: OS Outdoor Leisure Sheet 128 and 129 and Pathfinder 852 and 853

Public Toilets: In Melbourne

Refreshments: Melbourne Hall Tea Rooms and the Blue Bell Inn, Melbourne. The Holly Bush Inn, Breedon.

Pushchairs: Suitable only for the part of the route that runs alongside Melbourne Pool, half a mile all told but very attractive with lots of wildfowl.

☺ This is the church of St Michael which was built in the 12th century as a refuge for the Bishop of Carlisle. In those days the land north of the River Trent — Melbourne is just south of the Trent — was subject to attack by the Scots and, in fact, the first bishop had to take refuge here 190 miles from his cathedral.

☺ Inside the church there is an Australian flag to record that this village gave its name to the City of Melbourne, Australia.

1. **From the church, walk past Melbourne Hall Tea Rooms and turn right into Blackhall Lane. Follow this to a bridge.**

Q: What is the name of the tall trees on the left-hand side of the road as you approach the bridge?

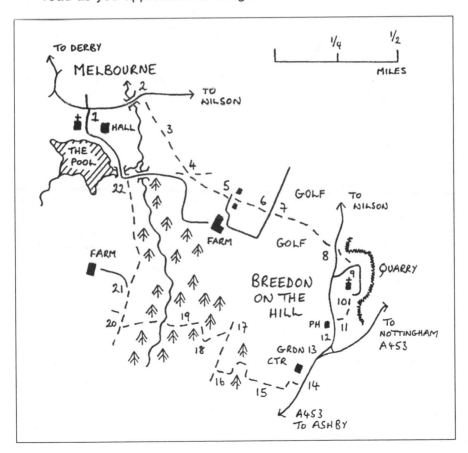

A: They are poplars.

2.   **Cross the bridge and turn right through a kissing gate. Now head diagonally left, through the trees to a stile in the top end of the opposing hedge.**
     (This area is often used for cattle grazing and can sometimes be subdivided by temporary fences.)

☺ When you are between the lines of lime trees take a look to your right and you will see Melbourne Hall and its garden. The present hall was built in 1696, using stone from the ruins of Melbourne Castle, and is the home of Lord and Lady Ralph Kerr. Just inside the hall grounds you should see the top of a black and gold wrought iron summerhouse known as The Birdcage which was made by the famous Derby ironsmith, Robert Bakewell, in 1710.

3.   **Cross the stile into an arable field and maintain your direction, heading for a cattle grid.**

☺ Have you noticed the colour of the soil? It is red from the breakdown of the underlying red sandstone which is found in this area and throughout the Midlands. If the farmer has planted a crop are you able to identify it?

Escape route: Before the cattle grid, turn sharp right and follow the farm track to reach the kissing gate at point 22.

4.   **Cross the cattle grid and bear left to a stile. Cross this and proceed diagonally right to another stile. Now head for the house on the skyline – to the left of the farm.**

Q: Why do trees in this field have wooden frames around them?

A: To protect them from the grazing cattle who otherwise could eat the young shoots and damage the tree bark.

5.   **On approaching the house you should see another appear to its right. Near the front of the second house there is a roadside stile. Cross this and the road and pass through a gap in the opposing hedge. Continue straight ahead and then descend the arable field to a gap in the bottom hedge.**

☺ On the skyline in front of you is Breedon on the Hill church. The hill has been extensively quarried, giving the church a dramatic cliff top setting.

6. **Pass through the gap and cross the road, and the stile in the opposing hedge.**

☺ You have just crossed into Leicestershire. Have you noticed any differences?

7. **Follow the path across the golf course, again heading for Breedon Church. After passing diagonally in front of a house, the path is enclosed by hedges before reaching a roadside stile.**

Q: What is the name of the spot from which a golfer starts the game?
A: A tee.

8. **Cross the stile and the road to reach a path. Turn right and follow the path, which shortly bears left, up to a road. Here turn left following the road up to a parking area.**

☺ The view from the top of this hill is wonderful. You should see planes landing and taking off from East Midlands Airport which is 3 miles to the north-east. To the left of the airport is Donnington Park racing circuit.

Q: Before reaching the church you will see a tree with a seat all the way round it. What type of tree is it?
A: A very old hawthorn with many other plants growing around its trunk and branches.

9. **Follow the road to the far side of the churchyard and its main entrance.**

☺ There has been a place of worship on this hill for over 1200 years, and before that time the summit was fortified by Iron Age man.

10. **Take the path opposite the churchyard entrance, which shortly descends towards Breedon village. Follow the path straight down, ignoring all side paths. Near the bottom of the hill the path joins a house access track to reach Hollow Road.**

11. **Turn right onto Hollow Road and immediately left along Melbourne Lane to pass the Holly Bush Inn.**

Q: What is the name of the inn that you are passing?
A: It is the Holly Bush and the name is to be found on the lantern over the front door.

12. **Shortly after the inn, follow the right-hand road to the A453 (Ashby to Nottingham road).**

Q: As you pass the village green look to your right and you will see a line of poplar trees. Each tree was planted in memory of a local man who died in one of the two world wars. How many trees are dedicated to men who died in the First World War?

A: 13.

13. **Turn right onto the A453 and follow it past the garden centre.**

Q: Opposite the garden centre there is a milestone. How many miles would you have to walk along this road to reach Tamworth?

A: 18.

14. **Just after the garden centre turn right and follow the path around a small golf course. At the rear of this follow the wide grass path that climbs the slope.**

☺ The fields behind the garden centre are usually planted with soft fruits. If they are, can you identify the type of fruit?

15. **The path passes under power lines and shortly levels out. When your way is blocked by a willow coppice, turn right to find a path through the trees.**

Q: What everyday medicine was originally made from the bark of willow trees such as those found in this coppice?

A: Aspirin.

16. **On emerging from the coppice, turn left and follow the field edge to a path T-junction. Here turn right and follow the right-hand side of the hedge. When the hedge ends and restarts on your right, continue forward for about another 30 metres.**

17. **Here turn left and cross an arable field, keeping just to the right of the second power line pole (counting from your right). The path continues over the rise to a stile giving access to woodland.**

☺ You have just crossed back into Derbyshire. Often county boundaries follow something that can be seen such as a river, but here there is nothing on the ground to mark the boundary.

18. Cross the stile and descend diagonally right to another stile. Cross this into a field and aim for the stile in its far right-hand corner.

19. This stile gives access to woodland which contains a small stream. Cross this by means of a plank and gently climb to another stile. On crossing this, ascend the field, keeping a wire fence to your right, to its top right-hand corner.

20. Turn right across a stile and continue along an avenue of trees to a further stile.

☺ This area is known as Melbourne Parks and once was the parkland belonging to Melbourne Hall. The avenue of trees indicates that a horse-drawn carriage drive would have passed through this area. Unfortunately, only a small length of the avenue still remains.

21. Cross the stile and bear right to another in the far bottom corner of the field. Cross this, climb a few steps and turn right to follow a field edge and then that of a wood. At the end of the wood continue straight ahead over a series of hedge stiles to reach a kissing gate.

22. Pass through the gate *(the escape route rejoins here)* and turn left onto a road which runs alongside Melbourne Pool back to your starting point.

The Pool, Melbourne

☺ This is Melbourne Pool, a 8 hectare lake through which the mill stream or burn runs — hence the name Melbourne. Wildfowl gather here in great numbers. The water is particularly graced by swans and their signets. If you have any picnic left these feathered friends will happily finish it for you!

Other Places of Interest in the Area

Melbourne Hall and Gardens

The house admits visitors only on Sundays during August. The key attractions of the garden are a 30 metre tunnel formed from yew trees, and the magnificent wrought iron work. Telephone 01332 862502 for opening dates and times.

The Donnington Collection

At the Donnington Park Race Circuit, Castle Donnington, there is an extensive collection of racing cars. Telephone 01332 810048 for opening dates and times.

Melbourne and Breedon on the Hill Checklist

☐ A CIRCULAR SEAT

☐ A LIME TREE

☐ A WEIR

☐ A GOLFER

☐ AN AUSTRALIAN FLAG

☐ A RABBIT

☐ AN AEROPLANE

☐ A SWAN

☐ A FISHERMAN

☐ A COW

17. Monsal Dale

Thousands upon thousands visit Monsal Head to admire its view of the Wye Valley, which must be one of the finest and best known in Britain. The route includes that view but also samples the riverside woods and meadows, and the lesser known limestone uplands above the opposing bank. The river valley and its banks are a haven for birds and plant life. The uplands provide a wonderful panorama and an insight into the realities of hill farming, a struggle against the elements.

Starting point:	White Lodge car park (SK171 706). The car park is situated 4 miles north-west of Bakewell on the A6.
By bus:	Services from Sheffield, Derby, Buxton, Stoke on Trent and Manchester.
Distance:	Entire route 3¼ miles
Terrain:	Upland track and riverbank paths. Steep climbs near the start and halfway through the route, but nothing too strenuous. Can be muddy along the river and around Brushfield Hough Farm.
Maps:	OS Outdoor Leisure Sheet 24
Public Toilets:	In White Lodge car park and at Monsal Head.
Refreshments:	Monsal Head Hotel and the Monsal View Café, Monsal Head.
Pushchairs:	Unsuitable

1. **Leave the car park by a short path, located mid-way along the length of the car park, that leads down to the A6 and, with extreme care, cross this to a squeezer stile. Pass through this, descend the stone steps and follow the path to stepping stones and a stile.**

☺ The caves and openings in the rock face near here were home to Stone Age man at least 8000 years ago. He would have hunted in this valley for food and clothing. Can you imagine such a life?

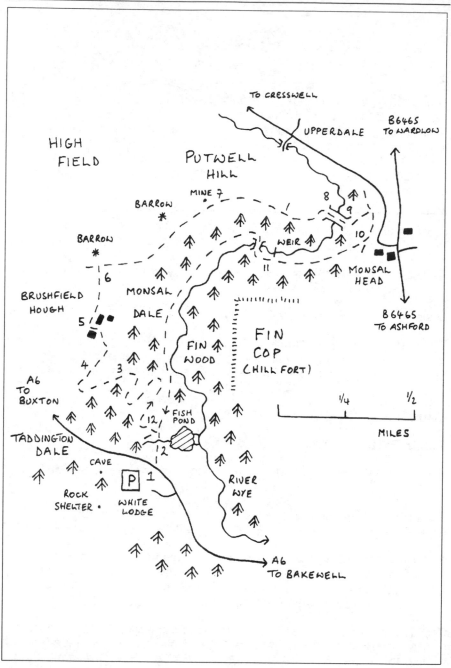

HIGH
FIELD

PUTWELL
HILL

TO CRESSWELL

UPPERDALE

B6465
TO WARDLOW

MINE 7

BARROW
*

BARROW
*

8

9

WEIR

10

11

MONSAL
HEAD

B6465
TO ASHFORD

6

BRUSHFIELD
HOUGH

MONSAL

DALE

5

FIN
WOOD

FIN
COP
(HILL FORT)

4

3

A6
TO
BUXTON

12

FISH
POND

12

TADDINGTON
DALE

CAVE

ROCK
SHELTER •

P   1

WHITE
LODGE

RIVER
WYE

A6
TO BAKEWELL

¼   ½

MILES

2. **Cross the stile and walk up to a junction of paths. Take the path signposted Brushfield and ascend the wooded hillside via series of steps.**

Q: What number can be found on the wooden signpost?

A: 1.

☺ The hillside that you are climbing is covered by a mixture of beech, hawthorn and ash trees as well as wild roses. Halfway up, and on your right, you should see an uprooted ash tree. It is still growing although it is lying on its side!

3. **On emerging from the woods continue along the path, which now has a gentler gradient, across shrub grassland. The path passes above Taddington Dale and then climbs to a wall stile.**

☺ On leaving the woods notice how the exposed limestone rock breaks through the soil here. In places you can see where weakness in the rock give access to the depths. (**DO NOT GO TOO CLOSE.**)

☺ To your right is Monsal Dale, and towering high above the other side of the dale is Fin Cop which has an Iron Age fort on its summit. Only the south and east sides of the fort needed to be defended as the other sides are sheer drops.

4. **Cross the stile and turn right onto a farm track. On approaching the farm (Brushfield Hough) you will see a "Private – No Public Right Of Way" sign. Here turn left to a small gate. Pass through this, a further gate and then turn left to a gateway between the barns.**

☺ This is a typical isolated, old upland farm. Life is hard here where everything is exposed to the weather. Snow settles early and lingers. Moss and lichen can be found on the stone, reflecting the weather conditions and the purity of the air. This farm scene is timeless.

5. **Turn right onto a farm track which follows the left-hand side of a long barn. Follow it through a line of extremely tall, slender and bare-trunked trees to a field gate. Pass through the gate and continue along the track through two fields to a track T-junction.**

☺ Over on your left, about 1½ miles away, you should see a village. This is Taddington, and at 1181 feet (360 metres) above sea level it is one of the highest in England. Near your path were found the graves of Saxon warriors who were buried with their swords and shields.

6. **Turn right and follow the track, which, after the second field gate, runs between drystone walls (the one on the right is broken in many places) above Monsal Dale.**

🙂 When the wall on your left ends, look in that direction to see a ruined building and churned up ground. This is an old lead mine. Many shafts were sunk in this area and the surrounding hill to reach and follow the veins of lead that run through the limestone. The miners spent long hours in these dark underground workings.

7. **When the enclosing walls end, continue along the track as it descends a grassy slope. When it turns sharp left, you should continue forward via a path which ends at a stile giving access to the Monsal Trail.**

🙂 Below and to your left is the picturesque and gorge-like Upperdale. Notice how the side valleys are heavily wooded but the uplands are virtually treeless!

8. **Cross the stile and turn right to Monsal Dale viaduct.**

Monsal Viaduct

☺ You are now on a walking trail formed from the trackbed of the old London to Manchester via Derby railway. Apart from passengers, the line was used to transport coal from the Derbyshire and Nottinghamshire mines to industrial Lancashire and to move vast quantities of limestone and other minerals from the local quarries. The line required demanding engineering work such as the tunnel and viaduct that you see here. The viaduct is some 24 metres high and originally had twin tracks laid on it. The now blocked tunnel is known as Headstone Tunnel and runs for approximately a third of a mile.

9. Cross the viaduct and follow the path uphill. Near the top you will meet another path. Here turn right and ascend to a wall gap, this gives access to Monsal Head.

10. Pass the gap and follow the lower path (nearest the fence) down to the river at a weir.

☺ You should hear the weir well before you reach it. The shallows below are a favourite paddling spot. If you are very quiet you may find that you are sharing it with some dippers. These black and white wren-shaped birds swim very well, despite not having webbed feet!

11. From the weir, walk downstream to a footbridge. Cross this, turn left and keeping close to the river bank, walk across the little meadow to reach the well defined path at the tree line. It is now a simple matter of following this path downstream for just under a mile (the path in places closely follows the river bank, and in others it cuts across the meadows) to reach the path signpost that you encountered at the start of the walk.

☺ As you walk downstream you should see squirrels, weasels, voles and other animals. The river teems with fish. Can you spot any? On the opposite bank lies the slope of Fin Cop. From here you can see why Iron Age man saw no reason to defend this side of his fort. At the edge of the meadows you may be treated to the delight of watching shaggy-coated cattle standing in the river shallows and taking a drink. In spring and early summer the meadows are a blaze of colour from their many flowers, particularly the Yellow Monkey flower.

12. Bear left to the stepping stones and retrace your steps up to the White Lodge car park.

Monsal Dale Checklist

- [ ] BRAMBLES
- [ ] AN OPEN-SIDED BARN
- [ ] A DIPPER
- [ ] CATTLE
- [ ] LICHEN
- [ ] WILD ROSE BUSHES
- [ ] A WEIR
- [ ] A BLOCKED TUNNEL

18. Osmaston Park

South of Ashbourne, the countryside takes on a softer image. Rugged hills give way to rolling agricultural land with hedges rather than drystone walls. This walk takes you through Osmaston with its thatched roofed cottages and around parkland, woods and lakes which used to form the Osmaston Manor Estate. The estate today is home to an abundance of wildlife.

Starting point: Osmaston Village Hall car park (SK200 439). Osmaston Village is 2½ miles south-east of Ashbourne and is clearly signposted from the A52.

By bus: Services from Derby and Ashbourne to Lane End crossroads, Osmaston. The lane leading to Osmaston is signposted at the crossroads. Follow this for just under half a mile to reach the parish church. Turn left to the Village Hall.

Distance: Entire route 3¾ miles

Terrain: Mostly tracks through undulating parkland, farmland and woods. A little village road walking, but mainly on pavements.

Maps: OS Landranger 128 and Pathfinders 811 and 810

Public Toilets: None, but the ones at the Shoulder of Mutton Pub may be used by customers.

Refreshments: Shoulder of Mutton pub, Osmaston

Pushchairs: Unsuitable

☺ **(AT THE ENTRANCE TO THE VILLAGE HALL CAR PARK.)** There has been a settlement here for over 1000 years but most of what you see today was built in 1849. The village was redeveloped to serve Osmaston Manor, which was at that time being constructed as a home for Francis Wright. Osmaston is therefore known as an Estate Village. The Wright family owned and managed the once great Butterly Iron Works near Ripley.

Coronation Cottages, Osmaston

Q: Opposite the car park entrance there are four cottages under
one thatched roof. They are called Coronation Cottages and
the plaque on the front of the building is dated 1937. Whose
coronation is celebrated here?

A: King George VI and Queen Elizabeth the Queen Mother.

1. **Turn right out of the car park and follow the village road past the
Shoulder of Mutton pub to the pond.**

☺ The village pond is home to mallard and domestic ducks, all of
which will be tempted by a morsel of food. On the far side of the
pond is a seat made entirely from horseshoes. Perhaps sitting in
it will bring you luck.

One of the thatched cottages here has its gable end facing you.
It is one of the oldest buildings in the village and you can clearly
see that it has a timber frame. The bricks are only there to fill in
the spaces and they provide no strength to the building. This
timber tent was one of the earliest forms of building.

2. **Turn left (keeping the pond to your right) and follow the road until
you reach the last house on your left. Here take the track marked**

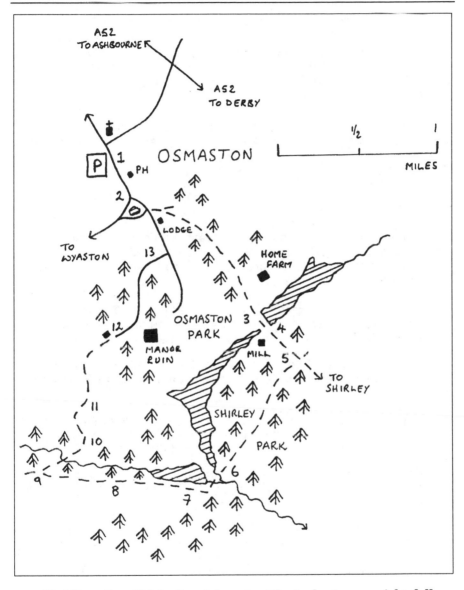

"Bridlepath to Shirley" and, keeping The Lodge to your right, follow it along and down to a lake.

Q: On the right just before you reach the first area of woodland you will see a single tree. What type of tree is it?

A: It is a very old oak tree. The exact age of the tree could be found by cutting it down and counting its rings. However, as we wish it to live a little longer its age can be estimated by measuring the distance around its trunk at about 1 metre from the ground. Each 2.5 centimetres equates to about one year's growth.

🙂 Notice the rhododendrons growing in the woods. These were planted when Osmaston Park was being laid out in the mid 19th century. They are now growing like weeds. The farmer is having to cut heavily into them just to keep the tracks open.

3. **On reaching the lake continue ahead, following the track to the abandoned saw mill.**

🙂 The lake to your left is home to many wildfowl. To your right the parkland is dotted with cedar trees. Can you identify them? They are conifers with bluish green needles and massive trunks and have a flat, wide-spreading crown.

🙂 The building on your right was a water-powered saw mill which was built in the style of buildings to be found in the Swiss Alps. Notice the huge water wheel that swings occasionally in the wind.

4. **From the saw mill continue ahead, following the slightly sunken track as it climbs the hillside to meet a junction of tracks and paths at its summit.**

🙂 The track that you have been following since Osmaston is a very old right of way. Over the years thousands of feet, horses' hoofs and wheels have cut the track into the hillside.

On reaching the end of the climb from the mill, look to your left and you will see a magnificent, tall conifer with a striking redwood trunk. Can you judge its height?

5. **Here turn right. (You will find two paths to your right. Do not take the one on your extreme right which should be marked "Private".) Follow the woodland track along and down for half a mile, to a ford. (Ignore all side tracks which should also be marked 'PRIVATE'.)**

🙂 This whole area is thick with pheasants. You will hear them scurrying through the undergrowth and, if you are quiet, you may see them in the open — they gather in numbers!

Q: Pheasants are not native to Britain. Where is their natural home?

A: Asia and Africa.

☺ As you walk along the track you should see further examples of the tall conifers with the striking redwood trunks. There are also specimen trees and shrubs which have been overtaken by the woods. Notice how the plants change according to light and soil conditions. Many trees are allowed to decay where they fall and this is witnessed by the abundance of fungi.

6. **Cross the stream by means of the concrete plank and bear left to another ford. Cross this and in a few yards you will reach a stile by a field gate.**

☺ To the right of each ford there are weirs and lakes. Often you will see heron fishing here.

7. **Cross the stile and bear right to follow the lakeside path (the lakeside is first clear and then hidden by trees and reeds) to a stile at a wooden fence.**

☺ These lake edges are home to many birds. See how many types you can spot. Look out especially for the swans that nest amongst the reeds.

8. **Cross the stile and two further ones, as the path continues parallel to the lake and then a stream.**

Q: **(POINT OUT THE BUSHES ON THE RIGHT JUST BEFORE THE SECOND STILE)** These are blackthorn bushes which bear purplish-black berries. What are the berries called?

A: Sloes.

9. **Shortly after the third stile you will see a field gate tucked sharply away to your right. Pass through this gate and take the tree and reed-lined track over the Wyaston Brook to another field gate.**

☺ Many of the trees in this wetland area are willows. Can you spot them? The willow's young, thin and relatively straight branches or "withies" are used for basket making.

10. **Pass round the gate and then follow the track, which bears away to the left and climbs to a gate and stile.**

11. **Cross the stile and continue along the track to a black and white house with a red roof. (Ignore the track that enters from the left.)**

☺ The tower which you can see above the trees is all that is left of

Osmaston Manor which was demolished in 1966. The tower is, in fact, a chimney for the manor's central heating boiler.

In this area keep an eye open for red grouse and other game birds.

12. **Follow the road past the house and bear left at the subsequent junction to pass a barn on your left. Continue along the road ignoring all side tracks until you reach a cattle grid at the edge of the woods.**

☺ In these woods you should be able to identify yew with its small, dark green needles and, in autumn, red berries.

Q: What early weapon was made from yew wood?

A: The long bow.

13. **Cross the cattle grid and at the road junction turn left to The Lodge. On passing this building, Osmaston pond is regained. Retrace your steps through the village to your starting point.**

Q: The road that you join just after the sports field used to be the main drive to Osmaston Manor. What type of trees form the avenue?

A: They are limes. They used to extend the full length of the drive, but most of them were destroyed by a gale in the 1960s.

Osmaston Park Checklist

☐ SLOES

☐ A FORD

☐ A THATCHED COTTAGE

☐ PHEASANTS

☐ A CEDAR TREE

☐ A TALL CHIMNEY

☐ CANADA GEESE

☐ HORSESHOES

☐ A CATTLE GRID

☐ SHEEP

19. Over Haddon and Youlgreave

Over Haddon and Youlgreave are old lead mining settlements built respectively above the sparkling waters of the rivers Lathkill and Bradford. The route follows the banks of those rivers between the two villages and returns across limestone uplands. The river Lathkill abounds with fish and wildlife, whilst the smaller Bradford travels through meadows which, in season, are carpeted with limestone-loving flowers. There are splendid views from the upland section.

Starting point: The pay and display car park, Over Haddon (SK203 664). Over Haddon is 2 miles south-west of Bakewell and is clearly signposted from the B5055. On entering the village, ignore the first right-hand turn, signposted to Monyash and Haddon Grove. Pass the Craft Centre on your right and at the T-junction turn right, following the main street to the car park.

By bus: Service Monday to Saturday from Bakewell

Distance: Entire route 5¼ miles. Escape route [A] 2¼ miles and route [B] 4¼ miles.

Terrain: Mostly river valley paths with some minor road and upland, grazing field walking. Steep but short ascents into Youlgreave and Over Haddon villages.

Maps: OS Outdoor Leisure Sheet 24

Public Toilets: Over Haddon car park and opposite the village hall, Holywell Lane, Youlgreave.

Refreshments: The Courtyard and Yew Tree Tea Rooms, Over Haddon, and Meadow Cottage Café, Youlgreave.

Pushchairs: Unsuitable

😊 Over Haddon is an old lead mining village. There are remains of mines all over these hills and dales. On the Ordnance Survey map you will see many abandoned shafts. Some mines do still operate, but they are now mainly concerned with the extraction of fluorspar or calcite. Fluorspar is used as a flux in the making of steel. Calcite is used in the manufacture of Portland Cement

1. **Leave the car park via the short path to the right of the toilets. On reaching the road, turn right and follow it down to the River Lathkill.**

😊 The source of the River Lathkill is approximately three miles from this point but in drought conditions the river bed here can be completely dry. At such times the ancient stone bridge and ford look very odd. The white house here, called Lathkill House, used to be the water bailiff's home. On the opposite side of the road are the remains of Sour Mill which ground corn from 1529 until the last century.

2. **Without crossing the river, turn left and follow the bankside path downstream. Shortly the path climbs a limestone outcrop. (In wet weather the stone becomes slippery.)**

😊 **(AFTER CLIMBING ABOVE THE RIVER)** If you look down to the river in drought conditions you will be able to see where its waters first appear on the surface. This point is known as Bubbling Springs. The Lathkill probably has the purest water in England and has ideal conditions for trout breeding. You will find that fishermen have to compete with the herons for their catch.

3. **Continue through a series of gates to reach river level and then a road.**

😊 The river has been formed into a series of pools by the construction of several weirs. Again this aids fish rearing, but it also creates a splendid habitat for wildfowl. Look out for the constant bobbing of the longtailed wagtails, kingfisher, coots with their soot black bodies and white beaks and various ducks. The river provides a lovely picnic and paddling spot.

4. **Here turn right to Conksbury Bridge.**

😊 This is Conksbury Bridge which was built in medieval times. It has massive stone walls and it carries the ancient track between Bakewell and Youlgreave.

Q: If you look over the downstream wall of the bridge you should see a number of wooden piers built out into the river. What purpose do they serve?

A: They are used for fly fishing. They save the fisherman from having to stand in the river wearing waders.

Escape route [A]: Turn back from the bridge and follow the road uphill to a sharp right-hand bend. Here take the steep path on the left and via a series of stiles, follow the valley rim to reach the road at the Lathkill Hotel. Turn left and follow the road to shortly reach the main street of Over Haddon, at the other end of which is the car park.

5. **Cross the bridge and follow the road for about 200 metres to a footpath on your left. Turn onto this path and follow it down through a series of stiles to a road.**

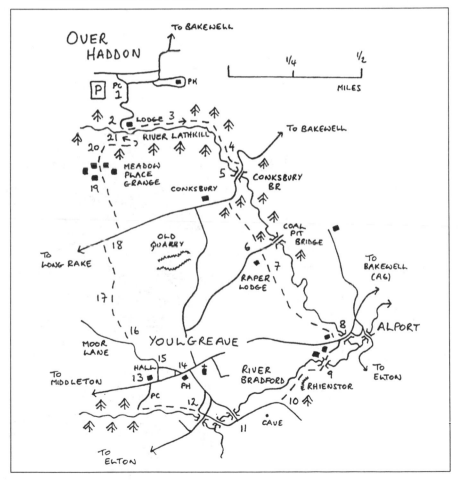

☺ The river downstream of the bridge is another favourite haunt of herons. Can you spot any? They stand so still whilst fishing.

6. **Cross the road and pass through the opposing squeezer stile to enter a field in front of Raper Lodge.**

☺ This is Raper Lodge which featured in the film version of D H Lawrence's novel *The Virgin and The Gypsy*. This famous Nottingham author lived for a time near here and the village of Youlgreave features in the same novel as Congreave.

☺ **(INDICATE THE RIVER BRIDGE)** This is Coalpit Packhorse Bridge which, as the name suggests, was mainly used for transporting coal from mines around Chesterfield.

7. **Continue forward following the right-hand side of a drystone wall downstream and through innumerable stiles to reach the main Youlgreave road at Alport Bridge.**

☺ The present Alport Bridge dates from the 18th century but this is a place of much older paths and river crossings. The village is built on the Portway, an ancient track which led from Derby towards Manchester. Without doubt there was a settlement here from as long ago as Roman times, if not earlier.

Escape route [B]: Turn left across the bridge and follow the main road to a road which climbs away to the left. Turn onto this and follow it to its end at a farm. Here bear left and follow the path to and over the Bakewell to Youlgreave road above Conksbury Bridge. You will shortly reach the rim of Lathkill Dale. Here turn right and follow the path through a series of stiles to emerge at a road in front of the Lathkill Hotel. Turn left to shortly reach the main street of Over Haddon, at the other end of which is the car park.

In the MOOd for a walk?!

8. **Cross the road and follow the drive to the right of the telephone box down to a bridge over the River Bradford.**

Q: What is the name of the cottage to your right as you walk down to the River Bradford?

A: Rhinestor.

9. **Cross the bridge and a stile to follow a path past the Rhinestor limestone cliff to another stile/kissing gate.**

☺ The 20 metre-high cliff is known as Rhinestor and it is a favourite spot for rock-climbers. It is great entertainment watching them slowly ascend the rock face by finding the smallest of hand and foot holds.

10. **Cross the stile to join a road which descends from the left. Follow this to where a footpath crosses a bridge and joins your road.**

☺ Just after joining the road and passing the first limestone cliff, look for a cave. These appear all over limestone country and the larger ones were inhabited by Stone Age man.

☺ **(AT THE BRIDGE)** The ancient way up to Youlgreave can still be seen from this one-arched packhorse bridge. Don't you think that the seat here has a wonderful natural shelter?

11. **Continue along the riverside path that shortly swings right and crosses the river to reach the Youlgreave to Elton road. Cross this and continue forward to a handgate beside a red telephone box and clapper bridge.**

☺ **(INDICATE THE BRIDGE)** This type of bridge is called a clapper bridge. It is made of huge stones and is extremely old.

12. **Pass through the gate and again follow the riverside path until you reach another clapper bridge. Here turn right and ascend Holywell Lane, past Meadow Cottage Café and the Village Hall, to reach Middleton Road at the Old Hall.**

☺ **(ON ASCENDING HOLYWELL LANE)** You are now entering Youlgreave (pronounced Youl*grave*), another lead mining village. The café on your left as you ascend the hill (Meadow Cottage) used to be the game keeper's cottage, and is one of only a small number in England that retains the "Teas with Hovis" sign.

Q: On reaching the top of Holywell Lane you will see a Wesleyan chapel. In what year was it built?

A: 1857.

13. **Turn right and follow Middleton Road to a little square in the centre of which is a cylindrical stone tub known as The Fountain.**

☺ This cylindrical stone tub is known as The Fountain but, in fact, it is a water tank which can hold up to 5400 litres. It is at the end of a pipe installed in 1829 to bring water to the village from a spring across the other side of Bradford Dale.

14. **Follow the road behind The Fountain which shortly joins Moor Lane in front of Old Hall Farm.**

Q: The building in front of you is known as Old Hall Farm. What is the date over the front door?

A: 1630.

15. **Bear right and follow Moor Lane out of the village. Continue until reaching a clearly defined, enclosed track on your right.**

☺ Isn't the view wonderful as you climb above Youlgreave? Can you see the television mast on Stanton Moor? See if you can also find it on the Ordnance Survey map?

16. **Turn into the walled lane (sometimes this can be rather muddy), and follow it to a field gate and squeezer stile.**

☺ The views get even better. On the horizon to the north-east you should now see the rock cliffs which follow the east bank of the River Derwent. Beyond these lies the county of Yorkshire.

17. **Pass through the squeezer and continue straight ahead, following the right-hand side of a drystone wall. When the wall bears away to the left again, continue ahead via a stile and up the next field to a squeezer stile just to the right of a field gate. Pass through this and within a few paces another one to reach the Conksbury Bridge to Long Rake road.**

Q: What do the road signs located either side of the road and to your left, mean?

A: Clearway — cars are not allowed to stop along this road.

18. **Turn right onto the road and then left over a wall stile. Walk straight**

ahead along the left-hand side of a field wall to another stile. Cross this and follow a similar line down to Meadow Place Grange farm.

☺ The farm in front of you is known as Meadow Place Grange. It belonged to Leicester Abbey from the 12th to the 16th centuries. In those days it was worked by monks.

19. Cross the wall stile and keep roughly straight ahead through the farmyard to pass between the barns via three gates. On entering the field on the far side of the farm, bear slightly right to a gate located just over the rise.

20. Pass through the gate and descend the woodland track to the River Lathkill.

Q: As you descend through the woods you should see a number of conifer trees which lose their needles during winter. What is this type of tree called?

A: A larch. Their light brown needles carpet the ground here in late autumn. Trees that lose their leaves or needles are called deciduous.

21. Cross the river and ascend the road back to your starting point.

Over Haddon and Youlgreave Checklist

- [ ] A DIPPER
- [ ] LEADED WINDOWS
- [ ] A CHURCH TOWER
- [ ] A RED TELEPHONE BOX
- [ ] A LARCH TREE
- [ ] A CAVE
- [ ] A STONE DOVE
- [ ] A FISHERMAN
- [ ] A STEEP HILL ROAD SIGN
- [ ] AN OLD STREET LAMP

20. Shipley Park

Do not be put off by the less than exciting approach to this country park. What was once a landscape ravaged by coal mining has been transformed into varied countryside which is pleasing to the senses. The park extends to 270 hectares and includes woodland, lakes, the remains of a country estate and old railway trackbeds.

Starting point: Visitor centre car park, Slack Lane, Heanor (SK432 453). The car park is 10 miles north-east of Derby and is signposted from the A608 on the outskirts of Heanor.

By bus: Service from Derby to the Jolly Colliers pub, Heanor. Then a three quarter mile walk down Thorpes Road (opposite the pub) and Slack Lane to the visitor centre.

Distance: Entire route 3¾ miles

Terrain: Mostly field, lakeside and woodland paths or tracks. A significant number of these have been built to an all-weather standard. Some walking on lanes but these have restricted vehicular access. Virtually flat.

Maps: OS Landranger 129 and pathfinder 812

Public Toilets: At the visitor centre and beside Osborne's Pond and Mapperley Reservoir.

Refreshments: The Ramblers Coffee Shop at the visitor centre

Pushchairs: Totally suitable

☺ This is Shipley Country Park which covers a former coal mining area. Visiting this spot before the 1970s you would have seen the pithead winding towers, coal being stored and transported by rail, road and canal; mountainous heaps of waste (slag) from the underground workings and even the earth being ripped apart to expose the coal for opencast mining. Everything would have been covered in coal dust. At one time thousands of men and boys worked here and the underground mines produced over

2000 tonnes of coal a day. The mines have gone, but during this walk you should see many interesting reminders of those times.

1. **Pass around the road barrier at the end of the car park (south-east corner) and follow the marked path down to Osborne's Pond.**

☺ This is Osborne's Pond which attracts many types of wildfowl. Here you should see great crested grebe which have the very pointed beaks and a neck ruff of feathers which is shed each year, various ducks, coots, Canada geese, swans and gulls.

Q: There are three types of swan. Those in this park are mute swans. Do you know the name of the other two types?

A: They are Bewick's and whooper swans. The mute swan is the only one with a red-coloured beak.

2. **On reaching the pond turn right and follow the shoreline path to Shipley Lane. Here turn left onto the road, follow it along the dam to the spillway and then walk up the embankment to the left-hand side of Hammers Bridge.**

Q: The pine trees along the north side of the pond do not shed their needles in winter. What name is given to trees that keep their foliage during the autumn and winter?

A: They are evergreens.

☺ Notice the water gauge just before you leave the pond. How deep is the water?

3. **Turn right to cross the bridge and follow the old railway track for approximately a quarter of a mile, until reaching a point just short of a path, with wooden guard rail, leading up to your left.**

☺ The wooded path that you are following used to be the trackbed of the railway serving the coal mines. The woods to the left of the path give way to small fields and the first of these often contains a number of horses and ponies. Carrots and the like are gratefully received but mind your fingers.

4. **Turn right and follow the path that curves left to climb the side of the old railway cutting. At the top turn right to follow the path in front of the two houses down to a road.**

☺ This little settlement is called The Field and is part of Shipley. Can you find the horseshoe on the second house that you pass?

Q: The open end of the horseshoe is kept uppermost. Why is this?

A: Superstition has it that if the open end is at the bottom of the shoe then your luck will run out!

5.   **Turn right onto the road and when it swings sharply to the right, carry straight ahead to follow Dog Kennel Lane past the entrance to a lakeside property (on your right).**

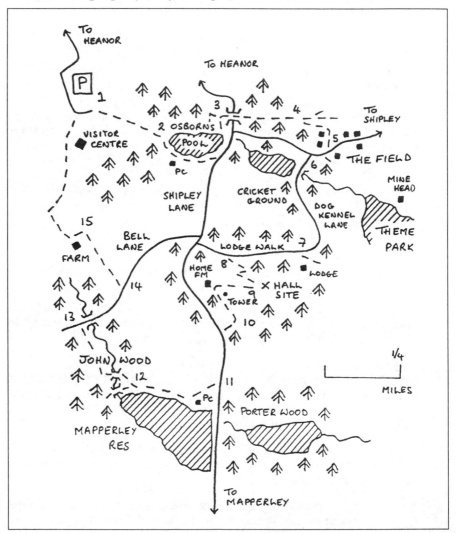

😊 Where a bridleway crosses the road, you should see the railway tracks that have been left in the road's surface. This is another part of the railway that used to serve the mines. The tracks followed the bridleway and if you look to your right you should see the old metal fencing that separated the tracks from the road.

6. **Continue along the lane, over a bridge and past the entrance to a cricket club (right). The lane now clears the woods and gently rises past The American Adventure Theme Park (left) to the foot of tree-covered Shipley hill.**

😊 Once clear of the woods you should have a view (left) of The American Adventure Theme Park. Notice the tall brick building with large spoke wheels at its top. This is the head of the shaft leading down to the old Mapperley Coal Mine. The wheels were part of the mechanism for lifting and lowering miners, coal and equipment to and from the depths. The lake was the site of Shipley Wharf from which coal was shipped in barges along the Nutbrook Canal and hence into the national waterways system.

7. **Follow the lane as it bears right at the foot of Shipley Hill to a junction below Nottingham Lodge. Continue ahead (i.e. ignore the way up and past the lodge) along Lodge Walk which follows the right-hand side of an estate wall to another junction.**

😊 The first building that you pass at the base of Shipley Hill is Nottingham Lodge. A lodge is the home of a gatekeeper to a country estate. Most buildings on a country estate had the coat of arms of the landowner marked on them. Can you find the coat of arms on this lodge? They are of the Miller-Mundy family who owned Shipley hall.

8. **Here turn sharp left and follow the signposted route to the Hall Site. The site is directly in front of the disabled car park (east side) and is picked out in bricks.**

😊 The site of Shipley Hall is beside the car park. The outline of the lower floor rooms have been picked out in brick. See if you can find where the front door, bay windows and main staircase would have been. The Miller-Mundy family were Lords of Shipley Manor from 1729, but they sold the hall to the coal mining company in 1944. The hall was then demolished as the mine tunnels had weakened its foundations.

9. **Return to the car park and follow the path up to a tower which is now a private residence. Here turn left onto Beech Walk and continue to a junction.**

☺ The tower is all that is left above ground of Shipley Hall – doesn't it make a wonderful home. Opposite is Home Farm, on top of which is a weather vane. Which way is the wind blowing?

Q: What type of very tall trees line the path behind the tower?

A: They are very old beech trees.

10. Turn right and follow the path down to a road. Turn left onto the road and follow it to a car park.

☺ As you walk down the road there is a view to your left of Ilkeston. Can you see its church tower? Beyond the ridge upon which Ilkeston stands is Nottinghamshire

The Tower, Shipley Hill

and the outskirts of Nottingham itself.

11. Walk through the car park and pass to the right of the toilets to reach the edge of Mapperley Reservoir. Here turn right and follow the shoreline path until it splits near its feeder stream.

☺ This is Mapperley Reservoir which was built over 200 years ago to supply water to the Nutbrook Canal. Like Osborne's Pond, it has considerable numbers and types of wildfowl but here there are more reeds for nesting. A birdwatching hide has been built in the reed area.

12. Take the right-hand fork across the stream and follow it through John Wood to Bell Lane.

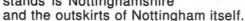

☺ This is John Wood. Notice that the type of trees change as you travel through the wood. Before you reach its end nearly all the trees are conifers – cone-bearing ones. Here you should see grey squirrels and even weasels.

13. **Turn right onto the lane and follow it to reach, in approximately 200 metres, a field gate and stile on your left.**

Q: What type of small trees or bushes line the lane?
A: They are hawthorns. The white flowers are known as "may" flowers.

14. **Turn left across the stile and follow the left-hand side of a fence to another field gate and stile to the right of Flatmeadow Farm.**

Q: When was Flatmeadow Farm built?
A: 1873. The date is shown on the front of the farm house.

15. **Follow the path round the farm, and then the old farm road back to the visitor centre car park.**

Other Places of Interest in the Area

The American Adventure Theme Park, Ilkeston

Hundreds of rides on the themes of the Wild West, Mexico and Space, including a roller coaster and river rapids journey. Telephone 01773 531521 for opening dates and times.

Shipley Park Checklist

- [ ] A SWAN
- [ ] A PITHEAD
- [ ] A HOLLY BUSH
- [ ] A RAIL TRACK
- [ ] GULLS
- [ ] A SPILLWAY
- [ ] A HORSE SHOE
- [ ] A CHURCH TOWER
- [ ] A PINE CONE
- [ ] A FISHERMAN

21. Stanage Edge

Of all of the gritstone cliffs (edges) that are an outstanding feature of the Upper Derwent Valley, Stanage Edge is the one with the longest continuous steep rock face. In all, it runs for some 4 miles and dominates the skyline north of Hathersage. The route takes you up and along part of Stanage Edge, allowing close inspection of the massive rocks and providing extensive, long-distance views of North Derbyshire. The walk also crosses the heather-covered moors behind the edge which in late summer are a sea of purple.

Starting point: Holin Bank pay and display car park (SK238 838). The car park is 8 miles south-south-west of Sheffield. Leave the city via Ringinglow and follow the road to Hathersage. Three miles from Ringinglow turn right towards Ladybower, and in the next half mile, right again for that destination. Within 200 metres the car park appears on your right.

By bus: Summer Sunday and Bank Holiday Monday service from Sheffield.

Distance: Entire route 2½ miles

Terrain: Moorland paths and tracks which can be boggy between points 5 and 6. Some walking along a moorland road. Young children will need close supervision along the edges.

Maps: OS Outdoor Leisure Sheet 1

Public Toilets: Located alongside the road 100 metres east of the car park entrance.

Refreshments: None

Pushchairs: Unsuitable

Stanage Edge

1. **At the rear of the car park follow the path up and through the trees to ascend the rock face.**

Q: There are often sheep grazing on the grassland next to the car park and certainly you should see them on the moors. Do you know what name is given to the yellowish, waxy material that comes from their wool and is used in soaps, toiletries and ointments?

A: It is lanolin.

☺ All around you as you climb through the trees, there are rocks that have split away from the rock face in front of you. Each winter, water entering cracks in the rock face, freezes into ice. The pressure exerted by the ice is so great that the crack grows bigger until the outer face falls away. Some of the fallen rocks are huge – can you imagine their weight and that they have been moved by natural forces.

☺ The paved path up the rock face is known as Jacob's Ladder, and you can see from the worn paving that many boots have passed this way.

2. **On reaching the top of the rock face, turn right and follow the edge top path to a broken drystone wall on your left.**

☺ There is a marvellous view from the top of the rock face. Below you is the Hope Valley and to the north-west are the heights of Kinder Scout and Bleaklow, both at just over 2000 feet (610 metres) above sea level. They are the highest points of Derbyshire and in the winter are often the first to be covered in snow.

3. **Turn left onto the path that follows the left-hand side of the wall and then crosses open grassland to a track. Here turn right onto the track and follow it to Stanage Pole.**

☺ The track that you follow towards a pole on the skyline is an old Roman route known as The Long Causeway. It was also the packhorse route between the Hope Valley and Sheffield. Packhorses were led by men who were called jaggers, and you will often see place names in Derbyshire which refer to these men, e.g. Jaggers Lane.

Q: The pole is known as Stanage Pole. What do you think it was erected for?

A: It was erected as a landmark for the packhorse trains. When these moors were covered with snow it would not be possible for the jagger to see the packhorse route. It was, therefore, necessary to have landmarks along the route which could be easily recognised and used for navigation.

☺ Stanage Pole also marks the county boundary. From it you have another view, but this time it is into Yorkshire and the countryside west of Sheffield.

4. **Turn right at the pole, passing around a "no vehicles beyond this point" sign and barrier, and cross the moor in a south-westerly direction to Stanage Edge.**

☺ Notice that this moorland lacks trees. This is due to the soil conditions and the wind. However, there is a thick layer of heather which turns into a vast purple carpet in late summer. The boggy areas support sedge grasses and in the dryer parts bilberry can be found. The blooms of this moorland attract bumble bees, which fly from one flower to another collecting nectar. The heather is home to red grouse and you should hear their calls.

5. On reaching the edge top path, turn left and continue until you notice the rocks on your right levelling out. Here walk closer to the edge and locate a path which descends to the road T-junction.

Q: As you walk along the edge top path you should see pools which have been formed in the tops of the rocks. What do you think has made them?

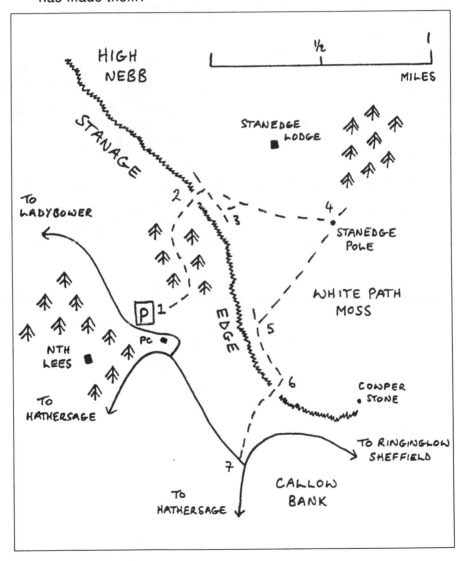

A: They have been made by the action of the wind and rain. Small
      grains of grit are continuously loosened from the rock's sur-
      face. Those that are not blown away become miniature grind-
      stones which are swirled around a point on the surface,
      gradually cutting a saucer-shaped cavity.

6.   **Follow the path down to the road. On reaching the road turn right
      and follow it to a junction just before a cattle grid.**

☺ From the road you have a view of Stanage Edge as far as High
      Neb, 1502 feet (458 metres). You should also see and hear many
      rock-climbers who appear as ants on the rock face. In the rock
      face (see map) there is a rock shelter known as Robin Hood's
      Cave. There is no proof that he used the cave but this area was
      at the north-west point of Sherwood Forest and Little John is
      claimed to have been buried in Hathersage Churchyard in the
      valley below.

7.   **Here turn right and follow the road for about 200 metres back to the
      car park.**
      *(A footpath at the rear of the toilets leads down a quarter of a mile to
      North Lees Hall. This is claimed to be the inspiration for Thornfield, Mr
      Rochester's home, in Charlotte Brontë's novel Jane Eyre. She certainly
      stayed at the parsonage in nearby Hathersage during 1845 and the Hall
      was owned by the Eyre family.)*

Stanage Edge Checklist

☐ BRACKEN

☐ A GROUSE

☐ OLD ROAD PAVING

☐ HEATHER

☐ ROCK-CLIMBERS

☐ SHEEP

☐ A HANG GLIDER

☐ A BUMBLE BEE

22. Swarkestone and Barrow Upon Trent

Swarkestone and Barrow are neighbouring small and ancient settlements on the northern bank of the River Trent. The route follows the river between the two villages and then returns via the Trent and Mersey Canal which hems them in to the north. Busy Swarkestone Lock is picturesque with its many brightly-coloured narrow boats.

Starting point: The Church of St James, Swarkestone (SK372 287). Swarkestone is 6 miles south of Derby on the A514. The church is located in Church Lane, which is the first road on the left after crossing the Trent and Mersey Canal from the Derby direction. There is car parking beside the churchyard.

By bus: Services form Derby to Swarkestone Bridge. Start the walk from point 2 of the route description.

Distance: Entire route 3¼ miles. Shorter route 1½ miles.

Terrain: Virtually flat. Riverbank and towpaths with some quiet road walking.

Maps: OS Landranger 128 and Pathfinder 852

Public Toilets: None, but the ones at the Crewe and Harpur Arms pub and the Swarkestone Lock Tea Shop may be used by customers.

Refreshments: Crewe and Harpur Arms pub, Swarkestone and Swarkestone Lock Tea Shop

Pushchairs: The shorter route is suitable

1. **At the main entrance to St James's churchyard (with your back to the church), turn left and follow the lane down to the River Trent. Now follow the river bank to Swarkestone Bridge and the A514.**

☺ This is the Trent, one of Britain's major rivers. It is approximately 170 miles long and its waters flow into the North Sea near Hull. The river enabled the Danes in 874AD to sail from the North Sea and raid Repton 5 miles upstream.

☺ The Trent, particularly when it was in flood, was a major obstacle to travel. Swarkestone Bridge was one of the few crossings and

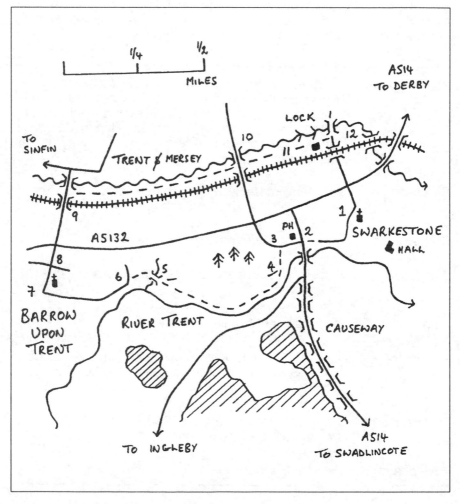

therefore of major importance. The original bridge was built in the 14th century and the three quarter mile causeway running south of the bridge dates from that time. In 1745 Bonnie Prince Charlie's Scottish army, which had marched south to attack London, gave up their fight here.

2. **With care, cross the A514 to Woodshed Lane. Pass the Crewe and Harpur Arms pub and follow the lane to where it turns away from the river.**
   Escape route: Continue along the lane to the A5132. Cross this to another lane, which shortly reaches a bridge over the Trent and Mersey Canal. Walk down to the towpath, turn right and follow the main route from point 10.

3. **Immediately after the first house on your left, you will see a pair of wooden gates signed Meadow Farm. Turn left through these and follow the path between houses to the riverside meadows.**

4. **The public right of way, on reaching the riverside meadows, bears off to the right, follows the south side of some woods and reaches the wooden bridge at point 5. This path is rarely walked and it is extremely difficult to find, let alone follow. Most walkers on reaching the meadows proceed directly to the riverbank, turn right and follow the fisherman's path to Barrow Upon Trent.**

Q: As you walk along the riverbank you should see small, white-painted and numbered, wooden stakes in the ground to the left of the path. What are these stakes for?

A: They indicate the places from which people can fish. Fishing along this section of the river is private and the fishermen have to pay a fee to the owner of the fishing rights. Some fishing places are more sought after than others as the fishes' interest in the fisherman's bait will be dependant on water depth, speed of the current, etc. Fish are very clever and wish to eat the bait without being caught!

☺ This being a fast flowing river, most of the wild life will be found amongst the reeds which line its banks. Waterfowl will seek protection in these areas and there you may see their nests, but do not disturb them. The little island in the river is a favourite nesting place for swans. Insect life also abounds in the riverbank areas. You should see damsel flies, and perhaps even their larger cousins, dragonflies, in all their brilliant colours.

5. **Approaching Barrow the riverbank path reaches a wooden bridge.**

(You have regained the right of way.) Cross this and continue along the bank, with gardens to your right, to meet a road.

Q: **(AT THE END OF THE PATH)** What is the black and white pole in the river used for?

A: It indicates the depth of the water. What depth of water is it indicating today? When the River Trent floods, its waters lap across this road.

6. Follow the riverside road, although the river soon swings away to your left, to the church.

Q: **(INDICATE TRENT HOUSE)** On one of the garden gate posts you should see a sun symbol plaque with the date 1710. What does this plaque mean?

A: It means that the house was insured against fire by the Sun Insurance Company in 1710. Firefighters in those days had no guarantee of being paid for putting out fires. They, therefore, would only attend fires where the house had such a plaque on them, which indicated that the insurance company would pay. There were several symbols for other companies.

7. Follow the road (Church Lane) as it swings around the churchyard to crossroads.

☺ **(OPPOSITE THE MAIN CHURCHYARD ENTRANCE)** The house opposite the churchyard entrance has a stone-walled enclosure attached to it. This is known as a pinfold and it was used to hold stray farm animals. The man employed to round up and oversee the animals was known as a pinder.

8. Walk straight across the crossroads and shortly you will reach the A5132 (Swarkestone to Hilton road). Cross this with care, turn right and immediately left into Sinfin Lane. Follow this, which shortly crosses a railway bridge, to the Trent and Mersey canal. Turn right and descend to the towpath.

☺ This is the Trent and Mersey Canal. It was built in 1777 by the Derbyshire engineer James Brindley to provide cheap transportation of bulk goods. It runs for approximately 92 miles between the Trent at Shardlow and Mersey at Preston Brook. It provides a navigational route between the North and Irish Seas and links with other canals.

Q: Each of the canal bridges is numbered. What is the number of this bridge?

A: 16.

9. **Turn right and follow the towpath to Bridge 15.**

Q: The path that you are following is known as a towpath. Why is it so-called?

A: Before canal barges were motorised they had to be towed (pulled) by a rope attached to a horse which would walk along this path.

☺ The double track railway line that follows the canal is usually busy with freight trains. They are transporting coal to the huge electricity generating stations located in the Trent valley.

☺ Look out for waterfowl, but they are limited by the wash of the boats and the use of diesel engines.

10. **Pass under bridge 15 and** *(the escape route rejoins here)* **continue along the towpath towards Swarkestone Lock.**

☺ The canal is used by many motor cruisers but the long canal barges can still be seen. These barges are known as narrow boats and they were specially designed for the canals and their locks. The narrow boats were also designed to provide a home for the boatman and his

Swarkestone Lock

family. Many of the boats are hand painted in bright colours.

11. **A kissing gate across the towpath marks the western boundary of Swarkestone Lock. Pass through the gate and continue along the towpath to the far end of the lock itself.**

☺ **(JUST BEFORE THE KISSING GATE INDICATE THE MILEPOST)** These mileposts were erected along the full length of the canal in 1819 and they show the distances to the two ends of the waterway.

☺ If a boat is coming through the lock you can see how it works.

12. **Turn right off the towpath onto Pingle Lane which passes under the railway to shortly reach the A514. Cross this and follow Church Lane back to your starting point.**

Swarkestone and Barrow Checklist

☐ A WILLOW

☐ A TRAIN

☐ A SWAN

☐ A NARROW BOAT

☐ A DAMSEL OR DRAGONFLY

☐ A MECHANICAL CRANE

☐ A FISHERMAN

☐ A ROW OF HOUSES WITH STABLE DOORS

☐ A MILEPOST

☐ A BLACK AND WHITE PAINTED HOUSE.

23. Thorpe

Thorpe village is located a few miles north of Ashbourne at the foot of the Pennine Hills. This walk takes you around this Danish named village and to Dovedale. The River Dove is crystal clear, well stocked with fish and bubbles its way through gorge-like scenery. It can be crossed by stepping stones which are a source of delight to children of all ages.

Starting point: National Park, Tissington Trail car park, Thorpe (SK165 504). The car park is 3 miles north-west of Asbourne. Follow the A515 Buxton road north for approximately one mile then turn left to Thorpe. At the Dog and Partridge pub turn right and in a few metres, when the main road swings away to the left, continue ahead and down into the car park.

By bus: Limited services from Ashbourne to the Dog and Partridge pub on Thursday, Saturday, Sunday and Bank Holiday Mondays. Follow the road opposite the pub to the car park as above.

Distance: Entire route 4 miles

Terrain: Mostly footpaths and tracks across grazing land. Some road walking.

Maps: OS Outdoor Leisure Sheet 24 and Pathfinder 810

Public Toilets: Dovedale car park, Ilam and Winter Croft, National Park car park, Thorpe.

Refreshments: The Dog and Partridge pub and The Peveril Of The Peak Hotel, Thorpe. The Izaak Walton Hotel, Ilam.

Pushchairs: Unsuitable

☺ This car park is built on the site of Thorpe Station. The railway line was built in 1899 and connected Ashourne with Buxton. Bridges, cuttings and embankments etc. were constructed to take twin tracks, but only a single track was ever laid. The line was little used and closed in 1971. The trackbed is now a walking and cycling trail known as the Tissington Trail.

1. **From the car park turn right onto the Tissington Trail and follow it, in the direction of Ashbourne, to a crossing path.**

☺ Nature has recovered much of the old railway line. Most of the trees that you see here are ash and in the autumn they are covered with a multitude of seeds.

Q: What common name is given to the seed pods of the ash tree?
A: They are known as keys.

2. **Turn right (path signposted Thorpe and Dovedale) through a kissing gate and into a grazing field. Walk up the gentle rise, aiming for the stile in the hedge just to the right of the power pole to which a transformer is attached.**

☺ Much of this area is devoted to dairy farming and a great deal of the milk is used by the Nestlé food factory in Ashbourne. You will probably see the Nestlé milk tankers travelling along the local lanes collecting milk from the farms.

3. **Cross the stile and continue forward to another one which gives access to the Thorpe to the Ashbourne road (Spend Lane).**

☺ **(AT THE STILE GIVING ACCESS TO SPEND LANE)** Notice that this stile replaces an old stone squeezer one. Squeezer stiles are to be found throughout Derbyshire. They consist of two large upright stones – rough hewn or worked – placed side by side to leave a very narrow gap shaped like a "V". Animals, particularly sheep, cannot pass through the lower part of the gap but people can by squeezing through – hence the name! Unfortunately, many of these squeezer stones have been removed or covered up.

The road that you are about to cross is called Spend Lane. "Spend" in Old English means "fenced strip of land".

4. **With care, cross the road and follow the lane directly in front of you to Broadlowash Farm.**

☺ **(AT THE ENTRANCE TO THE FARM)** You will probably see hens on and alongside the road here. They escape from the farm and their eggs are truly free-range. Ducks also roam here and are often followed by their brood of chicks, which can amount to no more than little balls of yellow fluff.

5. **Continue past the farm and follow the lane as it bears right, becomes sunken and descends to a culvert just short of a red telephone box.**

☺ As you descend the sunken lane, notice the wild roses that grow amongst the hedges and the many wild plants along the banks. In front of you are the first cottages of Thorpe village. It was named by the Danes when they occupied this area in the 9th century.

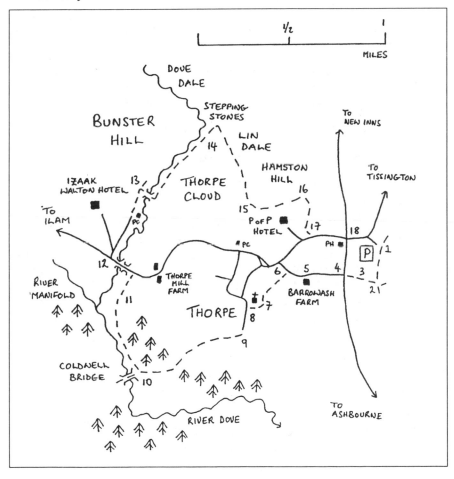

Q: Can you recognise the wooden building opposite Stoney
    Cottage?
A: Yes, it used to be a railway freight wagon.

☺ You cannot fail to notice, or rather hear, the geese kept alongside
   the road! Wouldn't they make good guards?

6. **Without crossing the culvert, turn left and follow the sometimes
    muddy path to cross the infant water course via a plank. Continue
    along the path, which shortly crosses a sidestream and then climbs,
    between drystone walls, to Thorpe churchyard.**

☺ Along the little water courses here you will see plants that only
   thrive in boggy conditions. Notice in particular the plants with
   large leaves that look similar to rhubarb. They are butterbur
   plants.

7. **Here turn right and then enter the churchyard via a hand gate. Follow
    the churchyard path to the entrance porch and then turn sharp left
    to reach a sundial.**

☺ This is the 12th-century church of St Leonard's. The stone pillars
   of the church door (inside the porch) have deep groves cut into
   them. These are believed to have been made by boys sharpening
   their arrows. At one time they were taught archery (long bow) In
   this churchyard. The porch is framed by yew trees — long bows
   are made from these.

   (AT THE SUNDIAL) It is believed that this sundial was originally
   made for horse riders. It must have been moved here from
   another site as its stile is set for a location further north than
   where this church stands. Turning back notice the spikes above
   the porch, they were placed there to stop people stealing the lead
   from the church roof.

8. **Return to the church porch and turn left to the churchyard's main
    entrance. Pass through the gate, turn left and follow the road until it
    ends at a field gate.**

9. **Pass through this field gate and follow the well defined track as it
    bears right and descends the slope to a bridge.**

☺ This track used to be the old road from Blyth Marsh (Stoke on
   Trent). It was built in 1762, but abandoned in 1910 when the first
   motor vehicles took to the road and could not climb the slope into
   Thorpe.

Q: Soon after the start of a stone wall (to your left) you will see a milestone dating from 1822. How far is it to Cheadle?

A: 11 miles.

☺ **(AT THE BRIDGE)** This is Coldwell Bridge, spanning the River Dove and joining Derbyshire to Staffordshire. The width of the bridge gives an indication of the size of the old road. Today there is only a path left on the Staffordshire side.

10. Without crossing the bridge, turn right and descend to the riverside field. Follow the base of the rising ground upstream, until it appears that your way is blocked by a hedge. Here follow the left side of that hedge and you will find a way forward, by a thin strip of land (bound to your left by a stream), to a stile.

☺ From the riverbank you may be able to see many fish in the river including brown trout. Izaak Walton and his friend, Charles Cotton, loved to fish in this river. It inspired them to write the famous book *The Compleat Angler* in 1653.

11. Cross the stile and carry straight ahead to the Thorpe/Ilam road. Turn left onto the road and follow it across two bridges to a road junction at the entrance to the Izaak Walton Hotel.

☺ In crossing the second bridge (St Mary's) you have entered Staffordshire. Do you think it looks any different from Derbyshire?

12. Turn right and follow the roadside path past a car park to a gate and stile.

☺ In front of you is the entrance to Dovedale, which is guarded by two limestone hills. On the left is Bunster Hill and on the right you can again see Thorpe Cloud. The limestone was formed 330 million years ago from the remains of sea creatures when this area was under a tropical sea. Thorpe Cloud was a reef in that sea. "Cloud" comes from the Old English "clud", meaning "rock". These hills are at the southern end of a range of hills known as the Pennines. They run for some 170 miles northwards to Scotland.

13. Without crossing the stile, turn right to a wooden bridge. Cross this then turn left and follow the River Dove upstream to reach the stepping stones.

☺ If the river is not running over the stepping stones, they are a fun

The Stepping Stones, Dovedale

way of crossing the river. **Take care, as they get slippery when
wet.**

*(It is well worth climbing Thorpe Cloud for the view. The path starts at
the stepping stones. Where rock is recently broken away you may see
examples of the fossils that make up this coral reef.)*

14. **Continue a few yards upstream and then turn right to follow the
left-hand side of a fence, and then a wall running at the base of Thorpe
Cloud. Follow the wall up through Lin dale until it swings away to
the right. Here continue straight ahead to reach the edge of an old,
abandoned quarry at the base of Hamston Hill (the track here leads
to public toilets).**

Q: What warning is given when red flags are flown on Thorpe
Pasture and Hamston Hill (the high ground to the left on your
walk up from Dovedale)?

A: They warn that the rifle range just over the rise in Waddle is being used. You must not walk beyond the danger signs.

15. **Cross the track which leads away southwards from the quarry and
continue around the base of Hamston Hill. In a short while the path
runs parallel with the wall and fence at the back of the Peveril of the
Peak hotel.**

☺ Notice the monkey puzzle trees with their sharp pointed, triangular-shaped, overlapping leaves that grow at the rear of the hotel. They actually come from Chile and Argentina and have nothing to do with monkeys. They received this name when a long-forgotten gentleman at a tree planting ceremony said, "It would puzzle a monkey to climb that tree."

16. Continue to follow the left-hand side of the wall/fence until reaching a National Trust sign. Here turn right across a stile and two further ones plus a squeezer to reach Winter Croft Lane.

☺ The hotel takes its name from William Peveril who was given control over the High Peak area of Derbyshire by William the Conqueror in the 11th century. Look out here for squirrels that live in the grounds of the hotel.

17. Turn left and follow the pavement uphill to reach the junction at the Dog and Partridge pub.

☺ As you walk along the pavement look over the hedge to your left and you should see the rifle range mentioned earlier.

Q: What is the name given to the target end of a rifle range?

A: The butts.

18. Turn right and then left, taking the road for Tissington. This is Narlows Lane. When the lane turns sharp left continue ahead to Thorpe Station car park.

Thorpe Checklist

☐ A MILESTONE

☐ A MILK CHURN

☐ A WILD ROSE

☐ GEESE

☐ A RED PHONE BOX

☐ A MILK TANKER

☐ A SQUIRREL

☐ A RAILWAY FREIGHT WAGON

24. Tissington

Tissington must be one of the contenders for the title of prettiest village in England. Its buildings, predominantly constructed of local limestone, are in complete harmony with each other and the landscape. An air of timeless tranquillity is achieved, which is enhanced by its famous well dressing each Ascension Day. The walk encompasses the principal village sights and follows part of the old Ashbourne to Buxton railway which was converted to a walk and cycleway in 1971.

Starting point:	Tissington Station pay and display car park (SK178521). Tissington is 4 miles north of Ashbourne and is clearly signposted from the A515.
By bus:	Limited Thursday and Saturday service from Ashbourne.
Distance:	Entire route 2½ miles. Shorter route 1¾ miles.
Terrain:	Mostly on quiet village roads and along a dismantled railway track.
Maps:	OS Outdoor Leisure Sheet 24
Public Toilets:	Tissington Station car park
Refreshments:	None
Pushchairs:	Suitable only on the shorter route

☺ This car park is built on the site of the old Tissington Station. Can you see the remaining platform and the railway track gradient indicator (this is a white post with two arms located beside the retaining wall of the north-bound platform)? The arm on the left shows the gradient of the line towards Ashbourne. It has been moved here from another site as the line descends to Ashbourne but the gradient indicator shows a climb towards that town!

1.   **Return to the car park entrance and turn left. At the road fork bear left and descend past a triangular-shaped green (right) to the village pond.**

☺ **(AT THE GREEN)** The village of Tissington has five wells. These

Tissington village

are dressed (decorated) on Ascension day to give thanks for their never-ending flow of pure water. For over 600 years the village has maintained its water supply, even though others lost theirs. It is believed that the practice of dressing the wells started after the village was spared the Black Death (1348/49), but there is evidence that the practice of offering flowers to wells and springs pre-dates Christianity. The first of the village's wells can be found on this little green and is known as Town Well.

Q: Next to the pond is the Old School. When was it built?

A: 1837. The initials stand for Francis FitzHerbert.

2. **Turn right at the junction in front of the Old School and in a few metres follow the path right to the church.**

☺ This is St Mary's Church, which dates from 1100. The base of its tower has walls over 1.5 metres thick. As you enter the porch you will see the Norman doorway which is decorated with strange figures, as is the font inside. What do they look like to you?

Q: There are deep groves in the door pillars. What do you think has caused these?

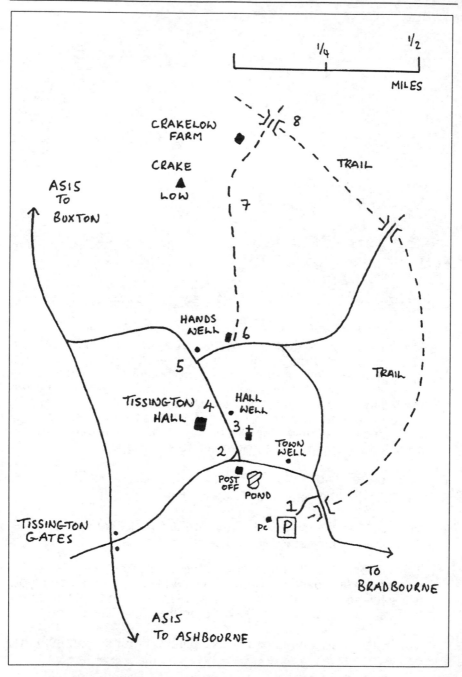

1/4   1/2
MILES

CRAKELOW
FARM

CRAKE
▲
LOW

ASIS
TO
BUXTON

TRAIL

8

7

HANDS
WELL   ■ 6

5

TISSINGTON   4
HALL

HALL
WELL

3 ‡

TOWN
WELL

TRAIL

2

POST
OFF   POND

1
PC   P

TISSINGTON
GATES

TO
BRADBOURNE

ASIS
TO ASHBOURNE

A: They are believed to have been made by archers sharpening their arrows. In the 14th century the boys of the parish were taught archery in the churchyard.

Q: In the churchyard there is a headstone marking the grave of James Allsop who died in 1912. Can you find it? How did he die?

A: He was a passenger on the ship called *The Titanic* and he drowned when it sank. Notice the odd spelling of drowned.

3. Return to the village street and turn right to reach Tissington Hall.

☺ This is Tissington Hall, the home of the FitzHerbert family since it was built in 1609. The head of the FitzHerbert family is a baronet and the family's coat of arms can be seen above the front door.

☺ Opposite the hall is another well. This one has a large hood and is known as Hall or Cup and Saucer Well.

4. Continue up the village street to a junction.

☺ At the road junction there is another well. This one is known as Hands Well and looks like a large tub or basin. To the right of the well you should see a very large water trough cut from a single piece of gritstone. Further examples can be seen around the village and they were cut in the quarries above Birchover (see walk number 3). Payment for these was made on the basis of 4½ old pennies (just under 2 pence) per gallon (4.5 litres) capacity.

5. Turn right and follow the road until you reach a footpath immediately after the last cottage on your left.
Escape route: Continue along the road to a junction. Here turn left and follow the lane for approximately a third of a mile to reach a railway bridge. Cross the stile to your right and descend to the trackbed, which is now the Tissington Trail. Turn right and follow this for two thirds of a mile back to Tissington Station car park.

6. Turn left onto the footpath and follow it past the cottage and straight up the hill by a series of stiles (squeezers and wall type).

☺ The summit of the hill is known as Crakelow which means "crows' burial mound", and the remains of Bronze Age man were found hereabouts. Don't you think the view is wonderful from here.

7. Continue straight ahead over the summit and then descend, by further stiles, to a field gate beside Crakelow Farm. Pass through this and follow the track to a railway bridge. Cross this and turn right over a stile to gradually descend to the Tissington Trail.

☺ **(AT THE BRIDGE)** The footpath and cycleway below you is known as the Tissington Trail. It runs along the trackbed of the former Ashbourne to Buxton railway line which was constructed in 1899. It was built to take twin tracks but never developed further than a single line.

8. Turn left onto the trail and follow it back to your starting point.

☺ The first cutting that you pass through is called Crakelow Cutting. It is a nature reserve maintained by the Derbyshire Wildlife Trust. The track-sides abound with wildflowers, wildlife and particularly butterflies. See how many you can spot. The cuttings show the limestone rock strata and how these have moved with time. Originally (330 million years ago), they were horizontal.

Tissington Checklist

- [ ] A HOUSE WITH A DATE
- [ ] AN ELDER TREE
- [ ] A COAT OF ARMS
- [ ] A DUCK
- [ ] A FONT
- [ ] A STONE TROUGH
- [ ] A TRACTOR
- [ ] A STATION PLATFORM
- [ ] A COW
- [ ] A CYCLIST

Games for Boring Journeys: 50 Questions and Answers

Some are easy, some are much more difficult. Most are mentioned in the text of the book. The answers are at the end of the section.

Derbyshire

1. Where in Derbyshire was Mary Queen of Scots held prisoner?
2. What was the name given to the men who led the packhorse trains?
3. Where in Derbyshire would you find the Cork and Cat stones?
4. What did the Romans mine in Derbyshire?
5. Where in Derbyshire would you find the Three Ships?
6. What is the most southerly English city supplied with water by the Derwent Reservoirs?
7. In which park would you find the Golden Gates?
8. Where in Derbyshire would you find an Australian flag in a church?
9. At which mill was cotton first spun using water power?
10. The rivers Goyt, Dove, Manifold Dane and Wye rise on a hill named after which sharp tool?
11. Name the Derbyshire town which is famous for its crooked spire?
12. Which friend of Robin Hood is claimed to be buried at Hathersage?
13. In which Derbyshire village would you find "Cup and Saucer" well?
14. Which famous haulage company started its business from a quarry now in Derbyshire?
15. What animal gives its name to an ingot of lead?
16. What nickname is given to Derby County football club?
17. Who is known as the "Lady of the Lamp"?
18. Name the Derbyshire town where a famous pudding was first made?
19. Which company's aero engines are made in Derby?
20. Which bird gives its name to a Derbyshire dale?

Nature

21. Which grows downwards – stalactites or stalagmites?

22. What is a female deer called?

23. How many claws does a robin have?

24. What is the name of the bird that eats pine-cone seeds?

25. On what plant would you particularly find a painted lady butterfly?

26. Name the small animal that tunnels underground leaving small heaps of soil on the surface?

27. From which tree do seeds called "keys" come?

28. What is the national flower of England?

29. From what wood are longbows made?

30. What is the name of the nocturnal animal with a black and white striped face?

31. What is a squirrel's home called?

32. To what species of deer does "Bambi" belong?

33. Which type of sheep have brown spotted fleeces?

34. The blackberry is the fruit of which plant?

35. Which bird is called by another word meaning fast?

General Knowledge

36. Name the port at the mouth of the River Mersey?

37. Where would you use a Davey Lamp?

38. Name the general who led the British army at the Battle of Waterloo?

39. What is the hardest natural substance?

40. Which elephant has the larger ears – Indian or African?

41. Whose mother lives in Clarence House, London?

42. Name the highest mountain in Britain?

43. Which river flows through London?

44. Which is the largest mammal?

45. Name the largest island of Europe?

46. Rome is the capital of which country?

47. Who was the first president of the United States of America?

48. Name the longest river in France?

49. What was the name of the first locomotive to pull a passenger train?

50. Name the Roman wall that runs from Newcastle Upon Tyne to the Solway Firth near Carlisle?

Answers
1. Chatsworth House
2. Jaggers
3. Stanton Moor
4. Lead
5. As part of Admiral Lord Nelson's monument on Birchen Edge
6. Leicester
7. Elvaston Park
8. Melbourne
9. Cromford Mill
10. An Axe
11. Chesterfield
12. Little John
13. Tissington
14. Pickfords
15. A pig
16. The Rams
17. Florence Nightingale
18. Bakewell
19. Rolls Royce
20. A dove
21. Stalactites
22. Doe or Hind
23. Four on each foot
24. Crossbill
25. Thistle
26. Mole
27. Ash
28. Rose
29. Yew
30. Badger
31. A Drey
32. Fallow
33. Jacob's
34. Bramble
35. Swift
36. Liverpool
37. In a coal mine.
38. Wellington
39. Diamond
40. African
41. The Queen's
42. Ben Nevis
43. The Thames
44. The whale
45. Britain
46. Italy
47. George Washington
48. The Loire
49. Rocket
50. Hadrian's Wall

Ideas for Games on Long Journeys

1. The game begins with someone stating. "I went to the shop and bought an apple." The next person repeats the above sentence and then adds another item e.g. "I went to the shop and bought an apple and an onion" . . . and so on. The winner is the one who can remember all the items in the correct order.

2. Pick a letter of the alphabet and see how many *living things* can be named using it as the initial letter. For example "C" – camel, canary and cow etc.

3. List some of the main towns on your journey and see who can spot the first road sign with the town's name on it.

4. See how many different words can be made from the following words:

ASPIDISTRA

DERBYSHIRE

CHESTERFIELD

CONSTANTINOPLE